MAKE
ALASKA
GREAT AGAIN

MAKE
ALASKA
GREAT AGAIN

'A CONSTITUTIONAL PETITION
FOR REDRESS OF GRIEVANCE'

CAPTAIN HENRY KROLL

Rev. date: 11/11/2019

To order additional copies of this book, contact:
Xlibris
1-888-795-4274
www.Xlibris.com
Orders@Xlibris.com
803952

CONTENTS

Preface

In order to fix something you have to identify the problem. Whenever a pocket of wealth is discovered somewhere, on earth like gold, oil, copper, etc., the scum of the earth show up to claim it. One way to claim this wealth is to become part of the government itself. Alaska now has the more state employees per capita than any other state. One in thirty people is currently drawing a state paycheck. ---2014 data.

1. <u>The number one thing that is wrong with his state is</u> Alaska is; it took resources away from land owners. All oil, gold, fish etc., etc. are claimed by the stat. Then they take in billions of dollars by leasing and selling those resources to large corporations. This creates boom and bust cycles. After the resources run out people go hungry and the corporations leave. New people coming to Alaska don't understand that the State owns the resources so they are inclined to allow the Legislature to put a tax on the labor and creativity of its citizens. An income tax would cost more to collect than it would take in and place even more of a burden on the poor and take food out of the mouths of children. We have to educate the people about this. We are 100% dependent on other states for almost everything.

2. Public officials have put us in danger of starving because only 2% of the food we eat is grown in Alaska. If there is a war or EMP in the lower 48 we are in trouble! Public officials violated their oaths to uphold the state constitution: ARTICLE VIII. NATURAL RESOURCES. <u>Section 1.</u> <u>STATEMENT OF POLICY</u> It is the policy of the State to encourage the settlement of its land and the development of its natural resources by making them available for maximum use consistent with the public interest. There are penalties for violating the oath of office but our corrupt legal system won't prosecute them.

Constitution of the State of Alaska

**ARTICLE VIII. NATURAL RESOURCES. <u>Section 1.</u>
<u>STATEMENT OF POLICY</u>**

It is the policy of the State to encourage the settlement of its land and the development of its natural resources by making them available for maximum use consistent with the public interest.

SECTION 2 GENERAL AUTHORITY

The Legislature shall provide for the utilization, development, and conservation of all natural resources belonging to the state, including land and waters, for the maximum benefit of its people.

SECTION 3. COMMON USE

Whenever occurring in their natural state, fish, wildlife, and waters are reserved to the people for common use.

SECTION 4. SUSTAINED YIELD

Fish, forests, wildlife, grasslands, and all other replenishable resources belonging to the State shall be utilized, developed, and maintained on the sustained yield principle, subject to preferences among beneficial uses.

Since Alaska was voted a state in 1959 our government representatives have allowed the destruction of several renewable natural resources either intentionally or inadvertently. In addition, Governor Walker took half of your dividend check and is trying to get the Legislature to approve an additional income tax on our labor.

If you have pledged allegiance to our flag I respectfully ask that you honor your pledge by helping stop this incredibly evil, dangerous, & growing "domestic" enemy. Remember Germany's unchecked corruption in the mid 1930's and early 1940's – and think of what the German public would have done had they known what was coming.

Alaska's state government was voted into existence by non-resident soldiers and non-resident agents and officers of corporations' intent on getting control of the resources to sell them for billions of dollars. Busses loads of soldiers circled around in a daisy chain voting two or three times. To give it the appearance of legality they wrote into the State Constitution that they had to set aside 25% of all revenues from the sale of oil and mineral resources in a Permanent Fund to compensate the people for the taking of their resources. They didn't create the Permanent Fund until after Jay Hammond became governor in 1974. We talked about the formation of the Permanent Fund in my living Room in Halibut Cove in 1973. The fund was created in 1976 and by that time billions of dollars had gone into the pockets of politicians and Swiss bank accounts.

To get control of the resources they also had to compensate the native inhabitants for the taking of their land with nine-hundred-million dollars and a state corporation. That put the natives under the control of state corporations to make them think they were getting benefits when in fact corporations are nothing more than commercial agreements on paper. It was like the Dutch buying Long Island for a handful of beads. The fact remains that this state still doesn't have clear title to any of its land and is operating in fraud. <u>Almost all property</u> is a quit claim deed subject to prior claims. This state government was doomed from the start.

Another danger we are facing is the fact that <u>only two percent of the food consumed in Alaska is grown in Alaska! There is no excuse for being completely dependent on other states for our food and everything else.</u> What if the US gets into another war? How will we survive?

1. We have to get more land into the hands of citizens so that we can feed ourselves in case something should happen to

the food supply in the lower forty eight. There is enough land area here, 93-million acres to form a self-sustaining country. However our government leaders have been so intent on ripping off resources and selling them that they have completely neglected the safety of the population. If there is a war or some other environmental catastrophe that interrupts the food supply in the lower states we will starve to death! This book will reduce the engineered recidivism used to grow bureaucracy. We have to finish the road to Nome that was planned and surveyed in 1944 to connect up to the Alcan Highway. The Governor to ask the President to build to defend the homeland. The Army could build it in 9 months. If the Japanese hadn't invaded Alaska we wouldn't have the Alcan Highway. It is of great military importance to defend this land and open it up so the people who reside here can get access to natural resources.

2. Harvesting resources is where original dollars come from; not service business. No state or country can exist very long without original dollars coming in. We have to build roads. It would not only open up the land so that individuals can mine gold, platinum copper, rare earths, cobalt, lithium, silver, uranium and diamonds. It would foster trade with Russia and be a tremendous boost to the tourism business and the economy of Alaska. At the end of this book are letters to Donald Trump, Lisa Murkowski and Don Young.

The following is from the Declaration of independence:

"He has obstructed the Administration of Justice, by refusing his assent to Laws for establishing Judiciary Powers.
He has made Judges dependent on his Will alone, for the tenure of their offices, and the amount and payment of their salaries.

He has erected a multitude of new Offices, and sent
hither swarms of Officers to harass out People, and
eat out their substance.
He has kept among us, in times of peace, Standing
Armies without the consent of our Legislatures
He has affected to render the Military independent
of and superior to the civil power.

He has combined with others to subject us to a jurisdiction
foreign to our constitution, and unacknowledged by our laws;
giving his assent to their Acts of pretended Legislation

CHAPTER ONE

The Corrupt Bastard's Club

This book started when I met a retired State Trooper who served during Governor Murkowski's Administration. Shortly after Murkowski left office Governor elect, Sara Palin tried to disband the infamous CORRUPT BASTARD CLUB. The FBI was called in and a number of prominent politicians were charged with crimes. Soon afterward Sara Palin was served with more than twenty-two lawsuits forcing her to relocate to Kingman, Arizona. She tried to clean up some of the corruption and set things straight but the Corrupt Bastard Club forced her to resign. (See a speech by Sarah Palin regarding this ugly history.) The governor's office was stolen from the will and vote of the people.

The same State Trooper informed me that the Alaska State Troopers were working with the CIA to bring drugs from Canada into Alaska. A newspaper reporter was jailed for reporting on this scandal.

After Bill Clinton left the governor's office in Arkansas the CIA could no longer fly coke and pot into Mena Arkansas from Panama. They had to find another way into the country. Apparently CIA flew the drugs into a remote Canadian airstrip. Small planes were used to hop over the border into Alaska. Some of the drugs were sold locally by the Troopers but the majority was smuggled via various air carriers with non-stop flights to Portland, Los Vegas and Reno etc.

Between 2003 to 2010 searches by airport security of passenger luggage and air freight leaving Alaska was practically non-existent. Nobody would expect drugs to be leaving Alaska so why would they bother to search? Greed and lust for big money selling off the people's resources by corrupt politicians got us into this mess.

HOW DID WE GET INTO THIS MESS?

Whenever a pocket of wealth such as gold, oil or gemstones is discovered somewhere on earth, the scum of the earth arrive to steal some of it. Whenever you have people earning two to six-hundred dollars a day in the oil field they become prime targets for dope peddlers. Where else are you going to sell dope—certainly not to poor people? Some, (not all) of the corporate heads of large corporations that were lured to Alaska by the State with tax cuts and rebates use cocaine and other drugs. They say it sharpens the mind. There are always a few bad apples in every bunch that see an opportunity to earn extra tax free dollars under the table selling drugs to their employees.

Alaska political corruption probe From
Wikipedia, the free encyclopedia:

According to Wikipedia the Alaska political corruption probe refers to a 2003 to 2010 widespread investigation by the U.S. Department of Justice, the Federal Bureau of Investigation, and the Internal Revenue into political corruption of nine then-current or former Alaskan state lawmakers, as well as Republican US Representative Don Young and then-US Senator, Republican Ted Stevens." According to Wikipedia, the investigation targeted what was sometimes referred to as 'The Corrupt Bastard's Club' or 'Operation Polar Pen. The investigation also focused on the oil industry, fisheries and for-profit prison industries."

Apparently Alaska's courts were putting innocent people in prison to benefit the pension plans of judges and other officers of the courts.

"In the spring of 2006, the FBI set up in a Baranof hotel suite just three blocks away from the capitol building in Juneau. It is alleged that from their position in the hotel suite, they gathered evidence, such as a videotape of VECO's CEO Bill Allen arranging paper money for legislators, and made other observations. The article goes on to say: 'By August 2008, the investigation resulted in indictments against six sitting or former Alaska Republican state legislators on corruption charges.' --Wikipedia

History of corruption probe:

Wikipedia states that the probe began in 2004 or earlier and by 2006 the name "Corrupt Bastards Club" (alternatively "Corrupt Bastards Caucus") began being used to designate Alaska legislators implicated in the federal corruption (a.k.a., "Polar Pen") investigation.

This author believes that the following charges against government officials were based on reports to the Alaska Public Offices Commission. This information is available to the general public.

- Senator John Cowdery (R-Anchorage), Senate Rules Committee Chair: $24,550.
- Representative Pete Kott (R-Eagle River), former speaker of the House: $21,300.
- Representative Norman Rokeberg (R-Anchorage), House Rules Committee Chair: $18,000.
- Representative Vic Kohring (R-Wasilla), House Oil and Gas Committee Chair: $14,708.
- Governor Frank Murkowski: $6,500 (excluding donations to past U.S. Senate races)
- Representative (currently Senator) Kevin Meyer (R-Anchorage), House Finance Committee Co-Chair: $12,300.
- Representative Mike Chenault (R-Nikiski), House Finance Committee Co-Chair: $12,000.

- Representative (currently Senator) Lesil McGuire (R-Anchorage), House Judiciary Committee Chair: $12,000.
- Senator Con Bunde (R-Anchorage), Senate Labor and Commerce Committee Chair: $11,500.
- Senator Lyda Green (R-Wasilla), Senate Finance Committee Co-Chair: $28,000.
- Representative Mike Hawker (R-Anchorage): $8,050.
- Representative Tom Anderson (R-Anchorage), House Labor and Commerce Chair: $8,000.

"The FBI who were in the Baranof hotel suite just three blocks away from the capitol building in Juneau were videotaped VECO's CEO Bill Allen, **peeling off bills for legislators** to stuff in their pockets. According to the Juneau Empire, Ray Metcalfe said he had spoken with FBI agents about the case, but didn't know how the feds first got interested in Alaska." I think the jury is still out on what started this," said Metcalfe."

This author learned that it was the Justice Department out of Washington DC that managed the investigation.

Wikipedia notes that, "...On August 31 and September 1, 2006 the FBI served some 20 search warrants in Anchorage, Juneau, Wasilla, Eagle River, Girdwood, and Willow, primarily on the offices of several legislators.

> The liberties of our Country, the freedom of our constitution, are worth defending at all cost and Thousand's died defending it in the past so it is our duty to defend them against all attacks. We have received them as a fair Inheritance from our worthy Ancestors: They purchased them for us with toil & danger & expense of treasure & blood: & transmitted them to us with care & diligence. It will bring an everlasting mark of infamy on the present generation, enlightened as it is, if we should suffer then be wrested from us by violence

without a struggle: or be cheated out of them by the artifice of false & designing men. Let us remember that if we suffer tamely a lawless attack upon our liberty, we encourage it, & involve others in our doom. It is a very serious consideration, which should deeply impress our minds, that millions yet unknown may be the miserable sharers of the event."

–Samuel Adams, U. S. Founding Father

We voted to move the capitol three times so why didn't they do it? Nooo-- they want to keep it in Juneau where people can't afford to travel down there and there is less oversight. When that forty-year-old pipeline starts springing leaks there will be nobody will clean it up! We must Make Alaska Great Again.

HATCH ACT

We need to start filing a complaint's with OSC.

The Hatch Act, a federal law passed in 1939, limits certain political activities of federal employees, as well as some state, D.C., and local government employees who work in connection with federally funded programs. The law's purposes are to ensure that federal programs are administered in a nonpartisan fashion, to protect federal employees from political coercion in the workplace, and to ensure that federal employees are advanced based on merit and not based on political affiliation.

How to File a Complaint

OSC is also authorized to investigate violations of the Hatch Act. 5 U.S.C. § 1216 (a)(1)(2). If OSC charges an employee with a violation of the Hatch Act, those charges are adjudicated before the Merit Systems Protection Board. 5 U.S.C. §§ 1215, 1504 – 1508, 7321 – 7326. Filers alleging a violation of the Hatch Act should use

Form OSC-13 (Complaint of Possible Prohibited Political Activity) to submit their allegation to OSC. Form OSC-13 can be printed from this website. Filers can complete the form online or by hand after printing the form. Once the form is completed it should be mailed or faxed (202-254-3700) to OSC. Please also include any evidence supporting your allegations (for example, documents, newspaper articles, photographs, etc.).

Please be advised that if the form is not filled out completely or the allegations are insufficient, OSC will require the complaint filer to provide additional information before it investigates. Accordingly, be sure to include all of the following information in the complaint:

Name and contact information of person who violated the Hatch Act ("Subject") Agency and position of Subject, Detailed description of the alleged Hatch Act violation, including names and contact information of potential witnesses and whether, for example, the election at issue is partisan (meaning the candidates are running as political party candidates)

In addition, for allegations involving a state, D.C., or local government employee, include:

> Information about the federal funding the Subject's
> employing agency receives
> Description of the duties the Subject performs in
> connection with federal funds
> Complaints should be sent to:
> Hatch Act Unit
> U.S. Office of Special Counsel
> 1730 M Street, N.W., Suite 218
> Washington, DC 20036-4505
>
> Fax 202-804-7002 hatchact@osc.gov

Enforcement

After investigating an alleged Hatch Act violation, OSC may seek disciplinary action against an employee before the Merit Systems Protection Board. When violations are not sufficiently egregious to warrant prosecution, OSC may issue a warning letter to the employee involved.

CHAPTER TWO

Alaska State Troopers, Judges & Law Enforcement

"The police must obey the law while enforcing the law." - U.S. Supreme Court Chief Justice Earl Warren (1891-1974) -

2/23/14 -The former commander of the Alaska State Trooper detachment based in Fairbanks was arrested Friday on charges of sexually abusing a minor over a period of several years. Former Capt. Warren Tanner, 75, was arrested Friday afternoon in North Pole by troopers and U.S. Marshals.

12/14/13 - Alaska wildlife trooper with traps on private land sued for trespass. The Alaska Police Standards Council voted to revoke state certification for five law enforcement officers and accepted the surrendered certification of four others at its Dec. 3 meeting in Anchorage. (ADN - Zaz Hollander)

12/9/13 - State revokes police certification for five, accepts surrendered certification of four others - Casey Grove ADN

5/19/13 - Panel will hear misconduct allegations against Alaska police officers - A state commission will meet behind closed doors Tuesday in

Kenai to decide whether a number of former police officers, troopers and corrections officers should lose their right to wear a badge in Alaska. - Kyle Hopkins ADN

1/18/13 - In early April 2012 the Alaska Commission on Judicial Conduct (Commission) referred to us its unanimous recommendation for removal of Judge Dennis Cummings, a district court judge in Bethel.

4/13/12 - Rollins Sentenced to 87 Years in Prison - An Anchorage Superior Court judge on Friday sentenced disgraced police officer and convicted serial rapist Anthony Rollins to serve 87 years in prison.

1/16/12 - How Alaska wildlife manager Corey Rossi was charged with illegal hunting. Someone in a trio of Outside men that former Alaska Division of Wildlife Conservation director Corey Rossi took on a bear hunt on the north side of Cook Inlet in 2008 is now in trouble with the law. - Craig Medred

8/11/11 - Alaska State Trooper Charged With DUI - See why it took two months to charge the trooper with driving under the influence. Police say he had an alcohol level more than five times the legal limit. - Alexis Fernandez KTVA

9/16/11 - Rollins Sentencing Set - A Superior Court judge has set former police officer Anthony Rollins sentencing date for December 2nd; Rollins was found guilty of 18 criminal convictions.

6-7-11 - Trooper charged with DUI in unmarked state vehicle. An Alaska state trooper has been charged with drunken driving nearly two months after police say he drove a state-owned SUV into two vehicles in Eagle River, court records show.

2/24/11 - Former cop convicted Tuesday faces 51 to 208 years in state prison. An ex-Anchorage police officer convicted Tuesday of sexually assaulting five women in 2008 and 2009 was earlier investigated on suspicion he was having sex on the job, the police chief said Wednesday. - Casey Grove ADN

SIX WOMEN: Ten counts include alleged attacks over three years; support agency first alerted police. -

2/23/11 - Former Anchorage police officer Anthony Rollins left court in handcuffs following his conviction Tuesday for four rapes while in uniform and on duty in 2008 and 2009. - Casey Grove ADN

2/5/11 - Ex-trooper: Town's police chief said he lied in first Waterman trial. A retired police officer testified for the defense Friday in the trial of a woman accused of telling two men to murder her mother, saying another officer working on the initial investigation broke procedure and told her he lied under oath during the accused woman's first trial. - Casey Grove ADN

1/29/11 - Ex-trooper loses job at Fairbanks courthouse; firing is alcohol related. FAIRBANKS — A retired Alaska State Trooper from Fairbanks with a history of alcohol-related arrests was fired from his job as a security guard at the Fairbanks federal courthouse last month for allegedly drinking at a bar before his shift.

10/6/10 - Airport police investigate officer charged in prostitution sting - Airport police are conducting an internal investigation of one of the department's officers, whom Anchorage police cited in July for soliciting prostitution, according to airport Chief of Police Lauri Burkmire.

2/9/11 - Motion to suppress evidence in Lloyd DUI case is common action - The attorney defending former Alaska Department of Fish and Game Commissioner Denby Lloyd against a drunken driving charge filed a motion to suppress evidence expected to be used by the state against him.

8/10/10 - Fish & Game commissioner pleads not guilty to DUI - Alaska Department of Fish and Game Commissioner Denby Lloyd pleaded not guilty to driving under the influence and reckless endangerment charges Monday in District Court.

8/9/10 - Alaska Fish and Game chief arrested on DUI charge - Alaska Department of Fish and Game Commissioner Denby Lloyd is accused of driving under the influence.

5/12/10 - Soldotna police officer resigns. Sgt. Tony Garcia resigned from the Soldotna Police Department on Friday. Garcia left the force, in part, because of the negative publicity that followed an allegation against him, he said. By Andrew Waite | Peninsula Clarion.

4/21/10 - Soldotna police officer under investigation. SOLDOTNA, Alaska - An officer in the Soldotna Police Department is being investigated for possible professional misconduct.

4/9/10 - Ex-officer sentenced in porn case - WASILLA - A former Anchorage police officer has been sentenced to four years in prison after pleading no contest to attempted possession of child pornography and admitting he violated probation terms in an earlier child porn case.

8/21/09 - Officer gets public defender despite $100,000-plus salary- An Anchorage police officer accused of multiple counts of sexual assault will get a public defender despite his $100,000-a-year salary, at least for now, a Superior Court judge ruled Friday. - ADN Megan Holland.

7/16/09 - Cop pleads not guilty in sex assaults - Rollins' attorney entered not-guilty pleas to 14 felony counts, most involving rape or sexual assault, and to six misdemeanor charges of official misconduct. ADN Don Hunter.

7/15/09 - Anchorage cop sexually assaulted 6 victims, police say - An Anchorage police officer was arrested Wednesday on charges he sexually assaulted six women during a three-year period while on duty. And police say there could be more victims. KTUU.

12/29/09 Jury should hear trooper shooting case, judge says. When Alaska State Trooper Jesse Osborn shot and killed an unarmed man at a Kenai highway pullout nearly seven years ago, was he acting with a legitimate police purpose? That's a question that a jury likely will decide, under a recent ruling by a federal judge.

2/10/06 - State settles lawsuit in trooper shooting - Juneau Empire.

2/16/03 - Alaska State Trooper Arthur Jesse Osborn - Trooper known for history of aggression. Controversy follows officer who killed disabled man at pullout By Lisa Demer Anchorage Daily News Trooper Shooting - State Fails Duty to Alaskans by keeping facts under wraps.

7/14/09 - Trooper arrested for DUI was also speeding, had weapons - Police say a trooper who was arrested for driving under the influence was also speeding. Troopers are calling it a personnel matter and cannot release the details, but they say 36-year-old Trooper Derek Loop is still on the job. - KTUU.

7/13/09 - Trooper arrested for DUI in Soldotna - An Alaska State Trooper was arrested Sunday for drunken driving and weapons misconduct, according to the state Department of Public Safety and a Soldotna Police Department report.- KTUU.

8/28/08 - Trooper loses job after pleading guilty to felony - An Alaska State Trooper has lost his job following his conviction on a charge that he forged prescriptions to get narcotic painkillers, troopers said Wednesday. Anchorage Daily News Published: August 28th, 2008 12:49 AM.

8/27/08 - Trooper gets suspended sentencing after plea - A former Alaska State Trooper has received a suspended sentence after being charged with forging prescriptions for narcotic pain medications. - The Associated Press Published: August 27th, 2008.

8/22/08 - Trooper charged with forging prescriptions - Authorities say a Fairbanks-based Alaska State Trooper has been charged with forging prescriptions for narcotic pain medications. The Associated Press - Published: August 22nd, 2008 01:08 PM

7/29/08 - Hunting Laws Need Apply to All, Even Troopers - Craig Medred - Outdoors ADN.

7/27/08 Is Wooten a good trooper? - Palin's Ex Brother-in-law: Union says yes, but investigation found serious concerns. He's the governor's ex-brother-in-law, and his job as an Alaska State Trooper is drawing scrutiny in a way rarely seen except in cases of killings by officers. By Lisa Demer - ADN.

7/25/08 - Kopp steps down as Public Safety chief - Megan Holland - ADN.

New Public Safety Commissioner Charles Kopp Holds Press Conference

7/19/08 - Monegan Fired - Gov. Sarah Palin fumbled badly with the sudden and clumsy way she fired Public Safety Commissioner Walt Monegan. The 30-year veteran officer and former Anchorage police chief was quite popular in his ranks and said he'd never been told the governor had concerns about his performance.

7/18/08 - Monegan says he was pressured to fire trooper - Former Department of Public Safety Commissioner Walt Monegan on

Friday said that since Gov. Sarah Palin took office, members of her administration and family pressured him to fire a Palmer Alaska State Trooper to whom her sister was involved in a bitter child custody battle. - Megan Holland - ADN.

4/28/08 Homer jail guard investigated - Jailer choked suspect, report says; no charges filed - BY MICHAEL ARMSTRONG STAFF WRITER Homer News.

3/28/08 Wasilla police shot and killed a 42-year-old Big Lake man in a shootout Tuesday afternoon near Mile 2.7 of Big Lake Road. Troopers said John R. Rivera, 42, died when Wasilla police returned fire after Rivera shot at them with a hand gun. The names of the officers involved in the shooting are not being released pending further investigation by the Alaska Bureau of Investigation. By MATT TUNSETH/ Frontiersman Published on Wednesday, March 26, 2008 2:21 PM AKDT

7/29/10 Former cop sentenced to time-served for child sex abuse - A former Anchorage police officer convicted of child sexual abuse won't be going back to jail. At his sentencing Thursday, Judge Michael Wolverton of the Anchorage Superior Court said Sammy Cohen completed his jail sentence while waiting for his trial.

3/7/08 Judge grants mistrial for porn case - The trial of Sammy Cohen, a former Anchorage police officer charged with sexually abusing his daughter and possessing child pornography, was called off Thursday. ADN By JULIA O'MALLEY

3/7/08 - Sexual assault trial called off for former police officer (Sammy Cohen): A trial for a former Anchorage police officer accused of sexually abusing a minor and possessing child pornography has been called off. - The Associated Press.

2/27/08 - Wildlife official cited in illegal moose kill - 'MISTAKE': Mike Fleagle turns himself in, pleads no contest. By James Halpin - Published: February 27th, 2008 12:29 AM - Anchorage Daily News

2/23/08 - Natives in Aniak claim troopers use racial profiling - The Associated Press - Published Saturday, February 23, 2008

2/17/08 - Aniak wants [Alaska State] Troopers out (Like living with Big Brother) - February 17, 2008 - Jill Burke - KTUU TV

1/10/08 - Former cop re-arrested on child-porn charge. Bryan N. Herrera, 44, is charged with three counts of possessing child pornography. Investigators found nearly 5,000 images on his computer, according to a police affidavit filed in court. Anchorage Daily News - by James Halpin.

10/18/05 - Anchorage police officer arrested on child porn charges. ANCHORAGE, Alaska (AP) - A 12-year veteran of the Anchorage Police Department was arraigned today on four felony counts involving child pornography - becoming the second city police officer in the last four months to face such charges. Juneau Daily News.

9/28/07 - Trooper Colonel defends Spitzer - Alaska State Troopers are defending one of their own tonight, saying Eric Spitzer is a good trooper. Spitzer has been named in at least four excessive force civil lawsuits, three of them have resulted in the state settling. The jury sided with Spitzer in the fourth case. By Megan Baldino - Friday, Sept. 28, 2007- KTUU TV

9/27/07 - Reaction to excessive force settlement - Alaska State Trooper Eric Spitzer has repeatedly been accused of excessive force, allegations that have cost the state nearly $700,000. The latest lawsuit was settled yesterday for $575,000. By Megan Baldino Thursday, Sept. 27, 2007 - KTUU

9/26/07 - State Settles Another Lawsuit Over Trooper Excessive Force - ANCHORAGE, Alaska -- The State of Alaska has settled a lawsuit today concerning the use of excessive force by Alaska State Trooper Eric Spitzer. An attorney says its the third time the state has had to settle over Spitzer's actions. By Megan Baldino - 9/26/07 - KTUU TV

8/12/07 - Travis Taric Hedlund, age 30 of Soldotna, had assaulted three individuals at the residence. Alcohol was a factor. Hedlund was arrested for three counts of Assault 4th-DV. He was remanded at Wildwood Pretrial and held with no bail pending arraignment. Author: MJW0 Received Tuesday, August 14, 2007 8:14 AM and posted Wednesday, August 15, 2007 1:12 PM. - www.dps.state.ak.us.

11/22/04 - State Trooper arrested after allegedly assaulting his wife - 27 year-old Travis Hedlund, a Trooper with the Alaska Bureau of Wildlife Enforcement in Soldotna, was arrested Saturday without incident according to the Troopers. - KINY Radio Juneau News.

8/10/07- Alaska State Troopers arrested Junior Anthony, age 35 of North Pole, for violation of conditions of release. Alaska State Troopers Press Release.

5/10/07 - A Grand Jury in Fairbanks indicted Junior Anthony, age 35 of North Pole, on two counts of Sexual Assault II following his arrest on 5/5/07. Alaska State Troopers Press Release.

5/7/07 - Trooper charged with sexual assault - A local Alaska State Trooper is accused of sexually assaulting a 16-year-old girl while he was off-duty. Trooper Junior Anthony, 35, was arraigned Sunday on two charges of second-degree sexual assault. He was arrested at his North Pole home on Saturday. By: Margaret Friedenauer Staff Writer Published 5/7/07 - Fairbanks Daily Miner.

10/31/06 - Former Alaska State Trooper John Patrick Addis - On The Run After Murdering Girlfriend in Nevada, Found Dead In Guatemala. Bad Cop News.com

10/16/06 - State Supreme Court Finds Illegal Search By Fairbanks Alaska Police Wasn't Justified, Overturns Conviction - Bad Cop News

9/29/06 - Woman Awarded $250K In Excessive Force Lawsuit After North Slope Alaska Police Officer (Now A Detective With Palmer PD) Kelly Turney And Another Assaulted And Choked 16 Year Old Girl, Duct Taping Her Mouth - Bad Cop News

9/15/06 - Crazed Alaska State Trooper Uses Bulldozer To Destroy Man's Home During Stand-Off - Bad Cop News

8/10/06 - 3rd Arrest for Trooper, Charged Again With Assault - An Alaska state trooper already arrested twice for assaulting a former girlfriend and on administrative leave was arrested a third time Tuesday in Cordova and charged with assaulting another woman at a local bar. Clinton Songer, 30, in the most recent case is accused of pushing his ex-wife to the ground, causing her arm to bruise after she asked him to leave a bar where she was having her birthday party Saturday night. - Daily News reporter Megan Holland can be reached at mrholland@ adn.com. posted August 10, 2006.

2/9/06 - Alaska State Trooper Clinton Songer -arrested on domestic violence charges. - Juneau Daily News

7/28/06 - North Pole Alaska Police Officer William Perry Sentenced To Just 6 Months In Prison After Bribery Attempt In Witness Tampering Case

7/1/06 - Man Who Died in Scuffle At Jail was Fighting Cancer, family says - The family of a Fairbanks man who died after suffering a broken neck in a struggle with state correctional officers at an Anchorage jail says the man was frail and battling cancer. Kevin Fitzgerald, an Anchorage lawyer representing the family of Douglas Jensen, said Jensen's family, most of whom are in California, is considering a lawsuit against the state claiming the use of excessive force. By Megan Holland Anchorage Daily News.

4/26/06 - Former North Pole Police Officer Charged with Felonies Related to Witness Tampering and Interference with Official Proceedings. Media Advisory Office of Special Prosecutions & Appeals.

4/18/06 - Former Nome Police Officer Matthew Owens Sentenced to 101 Years In Prison For Killing Teen Girl While On Duty Bad Cop New.

2/10/06 - State settles lawsuit in trooper shooting - Juneau Empire.

2/16/03 - Alaska State Trooper Arthur Jesse Osborn - Trooper known for history of aggression. Controversy follows officer who killed disabled man at pullout By Lisa Demer Anchorage Daily News Trooper Shooting - State Fails Duty to Alaskans by keeping facts under wraps.

10/20/05 - According to the Associated Press, a 12-year veteran of the Anchorage Police Department was arrested today on four felony counts involving child pornography - becoming the second city police officer in the last four months to face such charges.

8/25/05 - A 34-year-old Ketchikan police officer (Jonathan Clouse) is charged with driving under the influence of alcohol and fourth-degree weapons misconduct while off duty. - Juneau Daily News.

8/17/05 - Ex-trooper gets 4 years for sex assault - Associated Press

8/15/05 - Former State Trooper Sentenced for Sexually Assaulting Three Aniak Women - State of Alaska Office of Special Prosecutions & Appeals.

6/3/05 - Trooper Assault Lawsuit Settled - Women get $1 million from State - Anchorage Daily News.

11/18/04 - Alaska State Trooper Daniel L. Scott - Trooper held on 11 criminal charges. Accusations include kidnapping, sexual assault and assault

6/27/05 - The wife of Anchorage police officer Sammy Cohen, who stands accused of sexually abusing a minor and possessing child pornography, says he is not guilty.

10/19/04 - Alaska State Trooper Eric Spitzer - $1 million plus awarded in excessive force arrest.

7/1/03 - Alaska State Trooper Todd VanLiere - Judge sides with family in hunting case - State trooper chastised for bullying, lying about hunting violation.

11/1/01 - Man files excessive force lawsuit against Troopers - FAIRBANKS (AP) -- A lawsuit has been filed against the Alaska Department of Public Safety and three Alaska State Troopers by a man who says troopers detained him unlawfully and used excessive force after he witnessed a Fairbanks bar stabbing in 1999. - Peninsula Clarion

1999 - ExNome Chief of Police Robert L. Kauer - KAUER CASE UPDATE - The Federal Wildlife Officer - Fall 1999

And that's only the small percentage that got caught!

The big fish are still out there!!!

CHAPTER THREE

Alaska Corruption And That's Just The Tip Of The Ice Berg… My Question Is, How Many Of Them Didn't Get Caught???

The above list of judges and troopers convicted of various crimes and corruption doesn't count the ones who got away! The Corrupt Bastard Club in Juneau profited royally for three decades until Sarah Palin became governor. They were so open about their corruption that they actually had baseballs hats printed with their logo and they had recorded a song. The scandal ran too deep and too dangerous to report by the news media. After Sarah took office she called in the FBI and fired some of the kingpins who were involved in the illegal drug trade.

When government agencies like the CIA are making huge profits you have to expect some kind of retaliation. They Corrupt Bastard Club started their revenge by filing 24-lawsuits against Sarah Palin forcing her out of office and to relocate to Kingman, Arizona. The people of Alaska were shortchanged by the loss of the only honest Governor we ever had and the drug business continued on as usual.

The current Governor and the outgoing Governor were both EXXON lawyers. **Are oil companies involved in the drug trade? Do bears poop in the woods? Have oil companies been involved** in the drug trade in other states? Why does big money corrupt? You can't jail a corporation because they don't have a body to put in prison so all the government can do is fine them. Why should we bring more of them to Alaska?

By Sarah Palin

The Corrupt Bastards Club. They said it. I didn't.

"In Alaska we had a group of politicos who chuckled as they dubbed themselves the "CBC," which stands for "Corrupt Bastards Club." But it was no laughing matter. I, and many others, took them on. We won. When I served as chairman of our state's Oil and Gas Commission, I reported on the cronyism of the chair of my own Party, who had been appointed by our governor to that same energy regulating commission.

The whistle blowing resulted in him receiving the largest ethics fine in the state's history. But that was just the tip of the oily iceberg. The FBI investigated Alaskan lawmakers for taking bribes from the oil industry in exchange for votes favorable to that industry, and politicos ended up in jail.* The lawmakers actually called themselves the Corrupt Bastards Club and even emblazoned the CBC initials on baseball caps they gifted each other – that's how untouchable they believed they were. But average, concerned citizens said, "enough is enough," and shook things up. Though some of the CBC members ended up in horizontal pinstripes, much of the compromised party apparatus stayed in power.

"I'll never forget standing at the podium during our state GOP convention and asking delegates to stand up with me and oust the status quo because the political environment had to change for Alaska to progress toward her manifest destiny as a more productive—and ethical—state to help secure our union. Only about half stood up. The rest looked around gauging the political winds and sat on their thumbs. Our federal delegation was incensed at me. Their influence resulted in much of the party machine staying put, but I'll never be sorry I fought it.

"Today, doesn't it seem like we have a Corrupt Bastards Club in D.C.? On steroids? It might not be as oily and obvious as its Alaska counterpart, but it's just as compromised because its members, too, are indifferent to what their actions mean for We the People.

I'm prepared to be attacked for suggesting this comparison of the D.C. political establishment with the CBC. But I call it like I see it. And lived it! The fight over defunding socialized healthcare, aka Obamacare, should have opened everyone's eyes to call it the same."

"Alaska-based oil companies that bribed politicians, engaged in racketeering for years, and - in collusion with corrupt politicians - engaged in a conspiracy to rob Alaska of its oil wealth - and still continue to do so to this day."

A report released Thursday by the U.S. Justice Department's Office of Professional Responsibility, the branch's internal watchdog, illustrates that the failure of federal prosecutors and FBI agents to disclose information about those predilections was glaring, and that analysis takes up a large portion of the 672-page report.

The people who pull the strings that run this puppet government didn't want to give the resources and land back to the natives. Is it so hard to believe that when billions of dollars are at stake that the shadow government (those who profit in secret unseen by public eye) would have hit men? Our beloved Governor has body guards and he probably has people that secretly do whatever needs to be done. What's fifty-thousand dollars for a hit man when billions are at stake? There will always be hit men.

Word on the street says Ted Stevens recently converted to Christianity immediately prior to his death and that he wanted to give some of Alaska's land back to it's original inhabitants. The powers that run this state didn't want this to happen so Ted had to be eliminated. You will have to your own google search on this subject. I cannot quote specific articles about how Senator Ted Steven was murdered or details about the plane crash due to the fact that I don't have copy write permission to do so. NTSB's findings say it was pilot's error. Hit men situated statically seated near Uncle Ted to make sure he didn't survive the crash.

New Study Lists Alaska among Top 10 Most Corrupt States

By MARY KAUFFMAN

Saturday June 14, 2014

(SitNews) Ketchikan, Alaska - A 2014 study in the Public Administration Review looking at the impact of government corruption on states' expenditures lists Alaska as among the 10 most corrupt states -- leading to the Alaska Democratic Party to allege members of the Alaska House Majority are corrupt.

The new study, *"The Impact of Public Officials' Corruption on the Size and Allocation of U.S. State Spending"* by The American Society for Public Administration, identifies factors that have been correlated with higher levels of corruption. These include isolated state capitals, legal systems with resource constraints and even those with abundant natural resources.

Defining corruption as the "misuse of public office for private gain," the authors of the study, John L. Mikesell of Indiana University Bloomington, and Cheol Liu of the City University of Hong Kong, note that public and private corruption can have a range of negative effects: lower-quality work, reduced economic productivity and higher levels of income inequality and poverty.

The authors argue that public officials' corruption should cause state spending to be artificially elevated. Corruption increased state spending over the period 1997–2008. During that time, the 10 most corrupt states could have reduced their total annual expenditure by an average of $1,308 per capita—5.2 percent of the mean per capita state expenditure - if corruption had been at the average level of the states. Moreover, at the expense of social sectors, corruption is likely to distort states' public resource allocations in favor of higher-potential "bribe-generating" spending and items directly beneficial to public officials, such as capital, construction, highways, borrowing, and total salaries and wages. The authors use an objective, concrete, and consistent measurement of corruption, the number of convictions.

In their analysis, Mikesell and Liu examined more than 25,000 convictions of public officials for violating federal corruption laws. Factors weighed included states' population, employment and income levels, as well as legal resources, degree of fiscal centralization, political structure and election cycle. Based on this method, the most corrupt states according to the study are:

Indexed with Population	Index with Employment
01. Alaska *	01. Mississippi
02. Mississippi	02. Louisiana
03. Louisiana	03. Tennessee
04. North Dakota	04. Illinois
05. South Dakota	05. Pennsylvania
06. Tennessee	06. Alabama
07. Alabama	07. Alaska *
08. Illinois	08. South Dakota
09. Montana	09. Kentucky
10. New York	10. Florida

The researchers explored two possible theories: First, higher levels of corruption should cause states' spending levels to be higher than they would be otherwise. Second, corruption would distort states' spending priorities in ways that favor bribes from private firms and others.

This study led to Zack Fields, Communications Director of the Alaska Democratic Party, to issue a press release in which he states, "Following the VECO scandal, Alaska legislators have drawn harsh criticism as they voted to give tax breaks to their private sector employers, push megaprojects that would enrich their own families, and cheat local governments by devaluing the TransAlaska Pipeline."

Mike Wenstrup, Chair of the Alaska Democratic Party, also commented on the study saying, "Alaskans are very suspicious of Sean Parnell's motives as he hands over our resource wealth to his former employers and Outside special interests."

In a press release, the Alaska Democratic Party alleged conflicts of interest in the Alaska State Legislature to include:

- Two state Senators who are Conoco Phillips employees voted to give billions of dollars in oil tax breaks to their private sector employers by supporting the Oil Giveaway. One of those Senators won election following a gerrymandering orchestrated by Sean Parnell.

- Governor Parnell fired an Alaskan so he could appoint Outsiders to the State Assessment Review Board, with the goal of devaluing the TransAlaska Pipeline on behalf of companies that include his former employer. Devaluation of the pipeline would allow oil companies to fleece local governments by tens of millions of dollars.

- Speaker Mike Chenault spearheaded gas line legislation for a project that would terminate in his district, where he owns an oil and gas services company that could benefit from contracts associated with the project.

- Senator Cathy Giessel pushed a bill to raise DMV fees paid by Alaskans, even though the fee hike wasn't necessary and the fees would enrich a Republican donor.

- Representative Lynn Gattis, is pushing for a Knik Arm Crossing project that would enrich her family. Gattis' family is the largest land owner near the proposed right of way. Gattis also obtained payments from the Mat-Su borough for railway right of way while she was serving in the Mat-Su local Government even though payments from the Borough violated conditions of agricultural subsidies Gattis was receiving simultaneously from the state of Alaska.

- Representative Eric Feige is pushing for state funding of the road to Umiat, a project that would enrich the company for which he wife works. Feige's wife's firm Linc Energy has said that state funding of the road is what makes Linc's project economical. Feige's wife's salary doubled and she was promoted at Linc after Feige was elected. Linc also acquired thousands of acres of oil leases at the terminus of the proposed road shortly after Feige's election.

Alaska is the most dangerous state based on its violent crime rate for the third year in a row, according to the latest crime statistics from the FBI. The rate of violent crime increased significantly in Alaska last year–going from 636 violent crimes per 100,000 people in 2014 to 730 violent crimes per 100,000 people in 2015. Following Alaska is Nevada (696 violent crimes per 100,000 people) and New Mexico (656 violent crimes per 100,000 people).

Law Street's annual slideshow of the Safest and Most Dangerous States ranks all 50 states based on their violent crime rates. Each slide details the violent crime statistics for every city in the country with available data and a population of 25,000 or more. The qualifying cities are listed from highest to lowest rate of violent crime per 100,000 residents for each state. The category of violent crime is comprised of murder, rape, robbery, and aggravated assault.

The above article was printed in 2014 but not much has changed since.

CHAPTER FOUR

My Experience

I was born in the small fishing village of Seldovia, Alaska February 1944. My mother, the Public Health nurse instructed my father, the Mad Trapper how to deliver me. It was a very reckless and brave thing for her to do allowing someone not trained to deliver a baby.

I grew up watching my father work on his floating salmon processor, Shrimp. I learned to row a boat at age five and attended Susan B. English grade school in Seldovia.

While attending University of Alaska in Fairbanks in 1962, Peter Berch and I started the university dog team. As an Electrical Engineer major I worked on the ionosphere research transmitter north of Condit Hall that measured the height of the ionosphere every hour by bouncing radio waves off from it. I set the time standard and changed the film in the 35 mm camera that took pictures of squiggles on the oscilloscope. The distance between the squiggles measured the height of the ionosphere. Every day I helped and another EE student put the 24-exposure film into an envelope and mailed it to some obscure office in Virginia. Later on I learned that this decade's long research was instrumental in determining the height of the ionosphere to calculate the range of the HAARP project transmitters yet to be built in Glenallen, Alaska and other places around the world.

That winter the temperature went down to -85 degrees Fahrenheit. We had to carry boiling five gallon cans of water down to our fourteen dogs each day and feed them some dried salmon. I had had enough of Fairbanks so the next year I attended Sheldon Jackson Junior College in Sitka. The mild climate was ideal with rain most of the time and only about six inches of snow.

Two year later we had a good salmon season so my wife who I had met at Sheldon Jackson and I attended bought a boat in Chicago and traveled the length of the Mississippi River and through the Inter Coastal Waterway to Brownsville, Texas. Brownsville was too hot so we traveled back north to Corpus Christi. I got a job as a marine electrician in the Corpus Christi shipyard wiring 165-foot oil rig supply boats for Argentina and attended University of Corpus Christi.

MY FATHER, THE MAD TRAPPER

Below is a picture of Henry "Hank" Kroll and his 1929 Curtiss Wright Jr.

In 1933 President, Franklin Delano Roosevelt bankrupted the country, closed down all most all gold mining and had the Federal Reserve issue debt notes that are basically IOU'S backed by birth bonds on your birth certificates thereby conscripting the labor of all citizens born in America. The government confiscated all the gold and put miners out of work so that they could be drafted into the armed forces to fight Japanese and Germans.

Henry Kroll tied his homemade, canvas canoe to the side of his plane and departed Valdez. He landed on the beach at Hones lagoon located across the bay from the town of Seldovia. He was the first person to land a plane in Seldovia. He pulled the slip-knot on the rope holding his canoe to the side of the plane and it fell off onto the beach. Several people witnessed this, thought that his plane had fallen apart after it landed.

The United States Marshall Jack Fields hired Henry Kroll on the spot. Henry was young and strong with a plane ideally suited to track down foreign immigrants who were living in Alaska illegally. Jack Fields had orders to round up all non-citizens and put them in jail until they could figure out who they were and what country they came from. In order to have World War Two, the United States government had to determine who the illegal immigrants and who might be spies sent from Germany.

Many people came to Alaska via fishing boats, halibut schooners and via the Alaska Steamship Company from California, Oregon, Seattle and other places. They liked the scenery and mild climate of Seldovia so much that they would jump ship and sleep under the spruce trees until they could find work. Some worked in the canneries while others hunted and trapped.

Henry never carried a gun when arresting unregistered immigrants. He'd sneak up behind them, put his finger in their ribs pretending he had a gun and tie their hands behind their backs. Then he'd take them to Jail where he'd play the banjo and sing to them all night. Since he had the only plane transportation to remote areas was not a problem.

My mother Lois graduated New York University and received a scholarship to train in pediatrics at Eden Borough Castle, Scotland. After interning in Harlem she worked for Frontier Nursing Service as a Kentucky Mountaineer delivering babies on horseback. I have a little book with pictures of about 200 babies that she delivered. I assembled a small 100-page book about her life that she wrote for the Ballard Senior Center.

One day she saw a little ad in a newspaper where they needed a Public Health Nurse in Seldovia, Alaska. She wrote back and was accepted. Upon arriving on Alaska Steamship Denali she met the outgoing nurse who willed her the cat and the boyfriend who happened to be Hank. The year was 1936. At the time it was unusual for a woman to travel by herself. She traveled by fishing boat to the towns of Kenai, Homer, Anchor Point, Port Graham and English Bay to administer shots for diphtheria and tetanus.

Lois Kroll noted that Seldovia had no fresh water supply and the town was getting its drinking water from numerous wells that also dotted the landscape along with nearby outhouses. The only people that weren't sick where those that drank at five local bars. Right away she called a town meeting to gather a group of men to put in a dam and water line from Fish Creek. From that time on Seldovia had clean water.

December of 1941 Hank and Lois were living in an apartment building above Jack and Susan English. Susan English worked in the Seldovia post office. On December 7, 1941 Hank happened to turn on his Zenith Trans-oceanic radio at the exact moment to pick up an urgent broadcast from Hawaii. Three hundred and sixty Japanese planes launched an all-out, attack on the naval base at Pearl Harbor lasting about two hours. The Japanese damaged 18 ships and 347 planes. More than 2,400 American died and more than 1000 were wounded. The attack galvanized the nation into an all-out, effort to defeat the Japanese. Hank and Lois were the first to know of the attack and ran downstairs to get Jack and Susan to listen and alert the town to the news.

During the spring of 1942 my father, Henry (Hank) Kroll cut down trees in Tutka Bay located across Katchemak Bay from the town of Homer. My mother and father lived on a floating raft called a wannegan. Pop grew up working in the logging camps of Oregon so cutting trees down with a whip saw and an axe was second nature for him. That was a time before one-man, chainsaws were invented. The chainsaws at that time were big two-cycle monsters that took two men to carry and operate.

My parents had purchased an old 40-foot boat called Sea Bird from John Granrose of Anchor Point. The Sea Bird was powered by a four-cylinder Redwing gas engine. The Redwing had laid high up on the beach several years and needed a lot of caulking and paint to make it float but it allowed them to travel to Homer, Seldovia and other places.

Henry cut all the logs into timbers on an old sawmill in Tutka bay and transported them to Seldovia on the Sea Bird. He stacked all the timbers on the beach and stick-piled them and poured diesel oil over them for a year to preserve the wood. My father used the timbers and planks to build a fifty-foot by 20-foot power scow they named, Shrimp. Things like nails, paint, tools, were hard to get during the war. Even food was rationed.

Many people in Seldovia thought he was nuts for building out of spruce because of its tendency to rot and they were convinced he would never finish it. It took two years of hammering, bolting and sawing but finally it was ready to launch. For one man to attempt such a project was a remarkable achievement in its own right and garnered Hank much respect among many of the local inhabitants. Imagine someone all by himself building the 50-foot scow on the beach. See picture above and below.

Try to imagine going into the woods in Tutka Bay, cutting down trees with a whip saw, dragging the logs to tidewater with a washing machine engine and cutting them into timbers on an old sawmill and then transporting tons of timbers to Seldovia to build something like this in two years. It was built back in "BC" (before chainsaws).

The Shrimp was ready to launch but Hank and Lois didn't have any money to buy an engine to power it. Out of the blue, Lois received an $800 check in the mail from the estate of an aunt who had passed away. They used the money to purchase a new, six-cylinder Chrysler Crown with a 3.9 to 1 reduction gear. It swung a 3-foot diameter prop and was a powerful enough to push the scow along at a top speed of eight knots. Later they installed a smaller four-cylinder, Gray Marine for auxiliary power.

While my father was building the Shrimp Charlie Nelson built the 50-foot Viking on the Beach at Seldovia. The Viking was later lengthened in Kodiak to 60-foot. Men were real men in those days.

My mother, Lois Kroll wearing her nursing uniform.
Below is a photo of my Mother on her horse 'Babe' in Kentucky.

Mother delivered more than 200 babies before she came to Alaska while working for the Frontier Nursing Service in Kentucky. She was Public Health Nurse for Ninilchik, Kenai, Homer, Seldovia and Port Grayham from 1936 to 1944 when she had me. She instructed my father what to so and he brought me into this world.

ME, Henry Kroll on my sand spit picture taken 1946
ATTACHMENT 8 ME 1946

CHISIK ISLAND

SAND SPIT

SAND SPIT

My father used my sand spit as an airport 12 + years

I was born on the Shrimp while it was anchored in Seldovia Slough February of 1944. At the time, the power scow was frozen in six-feet-thick ice. My Mother was the Public Health Nurse for Seldovia, Homer, Kenai and other villages. She arrived in Seldovia the year of 1936. After I was born she quit that occupation.

Below is a picture of me and my first boat that materialized alongside the Shrimp in the Seldovia slough after I dreamed it would happen. I was born in the Shrimp.

I learned to row right away and couldn't get enough of the freedom to travel around the slough at high tide. A couple days later Pop made me a slingshot out of a forked stick and large rubber bands. I tried shooting it a couple times on board the shrimp but lacked ammunition. I could barely wait to row over to a little beach where there were lots of small pebbles.

My brother Herb Kroll and I on the left with a 98 pound king salmon. Picture taken 1955.

That summer my father set a net by a large rock in Tuxedni Bay and gave me an old red trap skiff. He put a five horse Johnson outboard on the stern. I got it started the first time and traveled three hundred yards over to the net. I managed to take sixteen red salmon out of the net. My hands hurt and the outboard wouldn't start. I rowed over to the Shrimp and my father was amazed that I had caught so many fish. He didn't expect the net to catch anything where it was set inside the cove. I was crying and he felt sorry for me. He told my mother that he would pay me a dollar a fish.

After that he set the net in front of the scow so that I could pick it at low tide. I would catch eight or ten fish every day, wash the mud off from them and drag them over to the Shrimp. August came along and the red season was over. One later afternoon as my net was going dry I noticed it had an entire school of fish in it. I ran up to the tent frame where we were living and told mom. She came down to help me pick fish and told my father's crew when they came in the cove from fishing.

With the four of us working it was Midnight by the time we got the last fish on the scow. All of us looked like mud people. I made $365 dollars that season. Not bad for a little guy age five.

I built up lots of mussel that summer. The other kids in school never picked on me much because I could out throw them down and out wrestle any of them. I fished salmon in Tuxedni Bay more than 66 years. We spent one winter in Yakima, Washington and I ice skated every weekend.

At age 15 I learned to fly a plane with my father flying from Seldovia to Titusville, Florida. He purchased 160-acres on Merit Island, Floridia and another 40-acre parcel of waterfront property Indian River Slough. We spent four winters in Florida and I rode the school bus every day to Titusville High School. After school Herb and I used to catch armadillos' while walking the quarter mile to our house from the main road and bring them home. You had to be real quiet sneaking up on them and grab them by the back. They have sharp claws so you don't want to have your hands underneath. Once you picked them up after a while they realized you weren't going to hurt them so they would stop kicking. We'd bring them home and feed them canned milk. Their little ant eater tongs darted in and out lapping up the milk.

We got to watch the first missiles blow up on the launching pad from our front porch. Our home was located about fourteen miles north of Cape Canaveral. The name was later changed to Cape Kennedy.

After Kennedy said we were going to the Moon and do the other thing the government kicked everybody off the island. There were families that had lived there several generations. They hired Georgia land appraisers to appraise the land at low prices. Everybody had to join a collective lawsuit in order to get paid for their land. It took six years before my parents got any money out of their land.

My father bought a $50,000 Bell 47-G-2 helicopter and took flying lessons from ag-pilots in Yakima, Washington. After 30 hours of lessons he flew to McKay Creek to visit his adopted Indian family. Jess Jones and Matte were trapped in their home and starving because the whole area was flooded from heavy rains. The roads were covered with water. Henry gave them a ride in his helicopter to a Safeway store and landed in their parking lot in Pendleton, Oregon. After buying groceries he took them back home to McKay Creek and gave all the little kids rides in his helicopter. Decades later the Indians told stories about Hank Kroll's helicopter visit

Hank was very persuasive and somehow talked the boss of Sea Land Shipping into letting him land his helicopter on the end of one of their large Sea Land barges to ship to Anchorage, Alaska. A couple longshoremen rushed up to put chains around it and he had to fight them off. He tied it down himself with ropes and wrapped plastic around it.

Although it was well covered after arriving at Anchorage Hank discovered that salt spray water had somehow leaked down into the swash plate below the rotor blades. Those big barges are hundreds of feet long and over forty feet high but the spray from the bow plowing into the waves had traveled the entire length of the barge.

Hank took off, landed in a Safeway market in Anchorage and using a pay phone called the International Airport tower to get permission to land. He didn't have a radio in the chopper. He landed at his old friend Howard Fowler hangar Natak Air. Not long after he had landed another helicopter took off with the fuel hose still in one of the fuel tanks and beat itself to death on the tarmac. The two men inside were killed.

After attending University of Alaska, Sheldon Jackson College and University of Corpus Christi Texas I worked as a marine electrician constructing two 165-foot oil support ships for Argentina. I met my first wife in Sitka, Alaska while attending Sheldon Jackson College. Moths later the Magistrate, Jack English in Seldovia married us.

Later that spring we traveled to Halibut Cove in the little 28-foot diesel boat my father and had built looking for a place to build a home. We went dry on the beach near the University property and were cooking breakfast when Clem Tillion showed up wondering who we were. I fed him a couple fried eggs and mentioned that we were looking for a place to build ahome. Later Clem pointed out some vacant land inside the deep water mooring. We eventually settled there.

I went back to Seldovia and loaded a stack of lumber that was in our Seldovia home and carried it up the steep beach and stacked it in Halibut Cove. Back in Seldovia I started up my father's old sawmill and sawed up twenty-five logs that we had rolled up onto the log deck. After taking that lumber to Halibut Cove we had almost enough to build a 16 by 20-foot cabin. When my father discovered I had started up his sawmill he almost had a heart attack.

To operate the mille you stood about four feet behind that big circular saw and pulled a lever wired to an old auto transmission that fed the carriage into the saw and with the other hand and a string connected to the throttle of the old Buick car engine. If a big sliver caught on the teeth of the saw it could drive a big stake right through your heart like a spear. One looked at the edge of the blade and gave it just enough throttle so that it ran true and as the log was fed into the blade you had to give it more throttle or you wouldn't get strait lumber. The Buick was hard to start in the mornings so I hooked up a 12-volt battery to the six volt starter. No problem!

After the salmon season Pat and I purchased the wonderful 36-foot seine boat, Nightmare from Nig Lippencott of Seldovia. He was a retired sea captain. Nig used to run cannery tenders and piloted a schooner scow to transport rubble out to sea under the San Francisco Bridge after the big 1908 earthquake.

The Nightmare was incredibly fast and could carry many tons. I re-calked the entire hull in Tuxedni Bay and later used her to transport a heavy load of mining machinery to Anchorage for my father. I got sucked into the bore tide at Turnigan Arm. I thought I would lose the twenty or so empty oil drums I had lashed vertically on the deck but after much banging around they stayed put.

After the March 1964 earthquake Seldovia settled five feet and the canneries and board walk were under water on the big tides. The city fathers voted to have Urban Renewal. All the canneries were torn down and the entire waterfront was completely gutted. Pat and I winched a creosote piling up onto the deck of the Nightmare and towed several long piling to Halibut Cover to build a dock. We also loaded much lumber and timbers from the Wakefield cannery for our cabin and dock.

Pat and I were married in 1967 and my son Henry was born in the Seldovia hospital February 28, 1968. He is now 53.

I fished long-line halibut and used the Nightmare to transport plywood and lumber from the fledging lumber yard, Spenard Builders Supply in Anchorage to Halibut Cove. It was much easier to run the boat to Anchorage and load the lumber and insulation directly onto the boat at Henry Emard's dock in Fish Creek than driving to Anchorage, putting it on a truck and driving back to Homer and then loading it onto the Nightmare for the trip to Halibut Cove. If you did the latter you would almost wear yourself and the lumber out by the time you got it to Halibut Cove.

Commercial halibut fishing in those days was different from what it is today. We didn't depend on the government to save us and we didn't have rescue helicopters. We especially didn't depend on the Coast Guard because they always wanted to know how many life preservers you had on board and other stuff. Talking to the Coast Guard was a big waste of time if you were busy trying to plug the hole in your boat. If by chance they had a Coast Guard cutter in the vicinity they would want to be hero's by taking you off your boat, let it sink and file a report then give the report to the news media so they could get more funding for their government corporation. As hard-working commercial fishermen we had invested everything in our livelihood and could not give it up. We didn't want or need the government to get involved. We wanted to keep our boats because our livelihood depended on it.

I always carried a five gallon bucket of roofing tar and a half sheet of ½-inch plywood on board. If you hit a rock and put a hole in your boat you ran it to the nearest beach and went dry. Then you nailed a piece of plywood with tar over the hole and went back fishing.

We made sure that we had three working bilge pumps at all times plus a homemade hand pump that didn't depend on electricity to operate. If by chance the bilge pumps didn't keep up with the incoming water you pushed a canvas tarp under the bow working it back over the hole with pike poles and tied it tight to the rails until you could find a sheltered cove with a sandy beach to go dry. Then you nailed the plywood and tar over the hole.

We always carried a skiff with a small outboard on deck for a lifeboat and we had enough supplies on board to last a couple months.

KING CRAB FISHERMAN

After my father passed away in September of 1968 I rigged his power scow Shrimp to fish kind crab. In 1969 we could fish all winter out of Seldovia weather permitting. The weather usually allowed us to re-bait our pots twice a week.

Some days the temperature would drop to ten degrees below zero. The Shrimp had a cast iron coal cook stove which wasn't enough to keep us from freezing to death so I searched around for an oil heater. The only stove I could find was a space heater designed to heat a large house. I nailed it down in the corner of the pilot house and cut a hole in the roof for the stove pipe. The oil heater consumed about five gallons of diesel a day with the carburetor turned down to its lowest setting but it kept the small pilothouse at about eighty degrees.

Basically the Shrimp was a floating time bomb. It would never meet today's Coast guard standards. It had two fifty-five gallon oil drums for fuel tanks mounted aft of the engines. Every three or four years one of the drums would rust through and there would be two inches of raw gasoline floating on top of the bilge water. I'd start a small Maytag washing machine gasoline powered motor connected to a ½-inch bronze pump on the aft deck to pump all the gasoline off the stern and walk away in case it caught fire.

In those days it was not uncommon for a gasoline powered fishing boat to blow up in the harbor. Gasoline fumes from leaking tanks or fuel line are more explosive then dynamite. When the boat owner touches the starter button boom!

As a kid I remember looking out the window of our house in Seldovia after hearing a tremendous explosion to see pieces of lumber, water and other debris one hundred feet in the air. Also there was a man flying through the air like Superman. When Dez Gunderson pushed the start button for his engine the resulting gas explosion blew him out of the pilot house door a good hundred feet landing in the water. He survived with only minor bruises and burns.

You would not believe the tenacity, perseverance and guts of some of the early pioneers in the king crab fishery. In the early 1960's a 50-foot boat capsized in Shelikoff Strait. One crewman died. The skipper managed to get a radio message off before the boat capsized. He clung to the keel of the capsized boat with one arm and hung onto another crewman by his hair. The waves washed over the two men all night. Early the next morning they were picked up by another boat. The skipper went back fishing the next day but the crewman was hospitalized and never was the same afterwards and never went near the water again.

Kroll helicopter taking off from Tuxedni Bay. Note* Mad Trapper on tanks.

1965

In the 1960's we owned the only privately-owned helicopter in Alaska.

CHAPTER FIVE

The Mary M

The spring of 1970, my wife, Pat and I were admiring the old Mary M in the Homer boat harbor. I was daydreaming at the time and made an offhand comment that I would like to fix her up someday. You have to be careful what you wish for in your twenties because chances are it will come true.

The Mary M was built in 1929 and 1930 by Tacoma Shipbuilding for the Metsetch family to seine herring. At that time the herring fleet traveled from San Francisco Bay to Ketchikan, Alaska each year in search of herring. The Mary M a four-cylinder, Atlas Imperial built in Oakland California in 1927. The twenty-thousand-pound Atlas diesel developed all of 130 horsepower at 300 revolutions per minute. It was coupled direct drive to the propeller through a planetary reverse gear. To stop the boat one had to turn a large brass wheel on a vertical shaft in the wheel house that was connected to chains in the engine room that connected to a long square steel rod with a lump near the end. The lump forced large brake bands together to grab hold of a two-foot diameter drum aft of the Atlas engine that contained planetary gears. Once the drum was stopped the propeller shaft turned the other direction and if you were lucky water boiled under the stern and the boat came to a stop without taking out several piling.

Below is a picture of the Mary M in Port Townsend, Washington.

Thinking back over the 23-years I fished crab in Kodiak and Cook Inlet, it came to mind that I should write a few paragraphs about my amazing old boat. The old girl took us safely home through some of the most raging storms, freak waves and ice-building northeasters that you could never imagine.

The 4-cylinder Atlas engine had about 40% reverse when fully engaged so one had to be very careful to get the boat stopped before docking. I took out several piling before I got the hang of it. When I bought her the bulwarks were al beat to hell from crashing into docks and barges. The reverse brake shoes were worn out so the usual procedure was to have someone sprinkle Ajax the foaming cleanser on the planetary drum to cut the oil that splashed up from the bilge.

The Atlas swung a three-blade, 51-inch diameter prop with 41-inches of pitch mounted on a four-inch bronze shaft. The best part of the four cylinder engine was the sound it made. The sound when underway was wonderful. It had a four-beat rhythm that was very pleasant to listen to. I wish I had some recordings of that sound. The sound was different every day because the wedges that rode on the cam-followers that opened the injectors had craters worn in them. The four-beat rhythm went something like this; chika-puka-chika-puka. Some days it was robo-tussen-robo-tussen and other days baga-juga-baga-juga. Sometimes one cylinder would get more fuel than the rest causing it to have a syncopated beat—barack-obama-barack-obama etc., etc. If you go onto Youtube you can find some old Atlas engines and listen to the sounds they make.

The Mary M was small for a herring seiner (only 76-feet) and only had six bunks below decks ahead on the engine room. They were accessible through an enclosed stairway on the foredeck and a vertical hatch forward of the galley that led to the engine room. There were two more bunks aft of the wheelhouse for the captain and cook.

It took a large crew to pull heavy seines back aboard by hand. The Mario Puretic seine block hadn't been invented yet. Seiners had to have a large crew of twelve to eighteen men to pull in the net after a set. Since there were only six bunks in the bow of the Mary M with a 12-man crew the men had to sleep in shifts.

There is a long period of time that I know nothing about. It would be interesting to know what kind of service she did during World War II. Most all the large fishing vessels in Alaska were conscripted by the Army and Navy to patrol the coastline and transport bombs, munitions and supplies to the troops on the Aleutian Islands.

In 1950 she was acquired by the larger-than-life, sea pirate, Rocky Roswell who was a hard hat diver. By 1956 the decks and bulwarks were rotted but the hull was in pretty good shape. Rocky had her rebuilt at Maritime Shipyard in Lake Union who eventually became Marine Construction and Design Company or as we know it today MARCO. They removed the bulwarks and entire back deck replacing it with ten-inch-wide white cedar deck beams and new fir decking. They drove new oak stub ribs alongside the existing ribs and put the old bulwarks back on over the new ribs.

They also installed two new 600-galon fuel tanks in the stern. One main tank in the engine room held 800 gallons and the auxiliary tank held 500-gallons giving her a total fuel capacity of 2,500 gallons. She consumed less than one gallon per nautical mile giving her a range of 2,500 miles.

Every summer ten years in a row Rocky along with a crew of four jimmy mechanics/pirates traveled north to Nome, Alaska. An entire fleet of 130-foot landing craft barges lay submerged upside down in sixty feet of water. They had D-8 Cats and road graders chained to the decks.

You must realize that the Alcan Highway wouldn't have been built if the Japanese hadn't invaded Alaska. I didn't figure this out until a year ago but all that equipment under 60-feet of water meant to finish the road to Nome. The road to Nome had been surveyed in 1944 and a big storm had capsized the entire fleet of barges carrying equipment to complete the road. That's why the army never finished the 800-mile road to Nome to connecting it to the Alcan Highway.

Rocky would dive down and cut the chains holding the heavy equipment to the deck and the air and fuel in the tanks would allow some of the barges to rise to the surface. They flipped them upright with air bladders, pumped them out, and his crew of grease monkeys swapped parts around until they got a couple of the old 6-71 General Motors diesels running. With engines bellowing black smoke burning the ten-year-old diesel in the tanks, his crew would take one to Dutch Harbor. Most years Rocky would salvage a second barge and tow it behind the Mary M to either Dutch or Kodiak.

Rocky sold the 135-foot power barges for $100,000 apiece. After paying his crew, he sent half the money to his wife Roslyn who lived in Anchorage. To my knowledge, he never saw her but maybe once a year. He was free to drink and carouse all he wanted and she didn't care as long as the money kept coming.

Cordova, Alaska was Rocky's home town. After spending three months salvaging huge barges in the Bearing Sea off the coast of Nome he was ready to party. A party was usually a good three-day affair. Rocky seldom wore cloths except for a suit of red, woolen underwear that he wore under his diving suit. He didn't need cloths and he probably didn't have any aboard the Mary M. After arriving in Cordova he would walk downtown in his red wool underwear. After a couple days of carousing and wrestling around on various barroom floors his fly wouldn't stay buttoned.

Cliff Lacy, the Cordova Harbor Master told me this story. "The city of Cordova had hired a new cop. The town council briefed him on what to expect. When the Mary M arrived at the dock the new guy went down on the boat float to greet and talk to Rocky. He said, "Now Rocky we don't want any trouble so please don't raise too much Hell." Rocky grabbed him by the belt, climbed a telephone pole and hung him twenty-feet off the ground.

According to Cliff, the new city cop was up there most of the night screaming and hollering for someone to get him down. Someone finally climbed up the pole and cut his belt in half with a knife and he fell on the ground.

One time Rocky fished 1000 Dungeness pots ranging from Kayak Island to Cordova and delivered one load of 60,000 pounds of crab. The Mary M had a huge hold. During the winters Rocky used the Mary M to tow one of the barges he had salvaged between Seward, Cordova and Valdez delivering freight and vehicles. The State took over this run with its ferry system.

During one ill-fated pirate venture Rocky took one of his 135-foot landing craft to Icy Bay and stole a big load of logging equipment. Heavily loaded with cats and graders the barge flipped over in the gulf. One man drowned in the engine room. Rocky put on his canvas diving suit and along with three men swam ashore on Hinchenbrook Island. They built a fire and waited until a passing fishing boat saw the fire and picked them up.

One of the many boats Rocky salvaged was the 85-foot fish tender Merganser. It went dry on a pinnacle rock in Shuyak Strait and sunk in 220 feet of water. At the time she had a large load of fish on board. Two-hundred-foot, depth is a little too deep for a hard-hat, diver but Rocky went down and managed to fasten two lines on her. He tied a 58-foot limit seiner to one of the lines and the Mary M to the other. As the 20-foot tides to work it into shallow water, patch the hole and pump her out. As the tide rose up the line attached to the limit seiner broke pulling the Mary M down on its side. Rock was hesitant to start the Atlas lying on its side but he had no choice. With the much larger vessel hanging below her he slowly worked her into shallower water to where he could attach another line.

Rocky towed the Merganser to Homer where it lay in front of the Salty Dog saloon boat ramp nine months. I was living in Halibut Cove at the time and witnessed several young men scoop tons of rotten salmon out of the hold and shaft alley.

After surviving a lifetime of extreme danger salvaging boats off the sea floor and other pillaging Rocky was done in by a woman. He was playing cards in Kodiak's iconic Mecca bar and grill located near the harbor when a woman propositioned him. He was in no mood to socialize. His mind was on winning the game. He gruffly rebuffed her advances. Apparently she took it as an insult. Hell hath no fury like a woman scorned. She returned a short while later with a hammer and hit Rocky in the back of the head. He died a day later from a brain aneurism.

The Hillstrands' eventually bought the Merganser and Johnny had her towed to Lake Union in Seattle. When I ran the Mary M south to Seattle in 1974 I saw the Merganser tied to a dock near Gas Works Park.

A couple years later Johnny spent over $110,000 on the Merganser converting her into the Sea Wife. After the Sea Wife arrived in Homer Jonny took me on a tour of his engine room. It still had the old Washington main engine but the crab tank and plumbing were exceptionally well engineered. By that time I had spent an equal amount on the Mary M getting her ready for the crab fishery and I did most of the work myself. My engineering worked but it wasn't near as pretty as the plumbing in the Sea Wife.

After Rocky died the Mary M fell into disrepair. Several different people tried to fish her. One group of alcoholics abandoned her in Raspberry Straits. The engine wouldn't start because it had rust flakes under the check valves. They were too lazy and stupid to clean out the rust flakes. They didn't even bother to anchor the Mary M. They just got into their seine skiff and went to Kodiak. Three days later after they were sobered up someone told them the Mary M was still afloat. They got in the seine skiff and went back to Raspberry Strait. The Mary M had some water in the bilge but not enough to submerge the engines. The Atlas engine started right up and they got underway without incident.

While drifting up and down Raspberry Strait the Mary M had gone dry on several rocks damaging the keel. If it weren't for the fact that the main keel was a huge, full length 16-inch, fir timber such treatment would have broken the back of an ordinary boat.

The Morehouse's and then the Kilcher's tried to make money with the Mary M but none were dedicated enough to put the time and energy into fixing her.

After the 1973 salmon season a couple of guys even tried to burn her while tied to the float in Cordova. I know their names but can't mention them here because it might stir up repercussions among family members. Their first attempt at burning the Mary M was to cut the fuel lines leading to the aft tanks draining the diesel into the hold and lighting an old mattress on fire. Black smoke came billowed out of the open hatch so the would-be arsonists panicked and closed the hatch cover smothering the fire. They didn't want the fire department to see the smoke.

After the first attempt they copped four five-gallon cans open with a hatchet, filled them with gas and carried the open cans down the float to the boat. They sloshed the gasoline down the passage way to the engine room and threw a match through the Dutch door of the galley. This time the fire really took off.

Cordova has one of the best volunteer fire departments in Alaska. They saw the smoke and came running down the floats pushing a giant foam fire extinguisher on wheels. The two would-be arsonists met them on the floats repeating, "There's dynamite on board. There's dynamite on board." "Don't go on there."

The firemen brushed the two goofballs aside, went onboard and knocked the heavy planked forward hatch completely off its foundation. Donning scuba gear they entered the smoke filled crew-quarters, walked aft toward the engine room and put the fire out.

A year later I bought the Mary M in May of 1974. It seems to rain most the time in Cordova. The boat floats are covered with green slime. It was like walking on ice.

The Mary M had been burned to where there was over a ½ inch of charcoal on the overhead timbers in the engine room and there were four-inches of dried chemical fire extinguisher material on top of the four-cylinder main engine. The arsonists had thrown gasoline down in the engine room. The heat had blistered the green linoleum on the edge of the galley table.

When my wife Pat and I and our three children flew to Cordova to rebuild the Mary M.

All the wiring was burned to a crisp and the one-inch thick glass port holes above the engine room were cracked and broke. There was about four inched of chemical fire retardant on top of the engine. Four square, five-gallon empty gas cans were sitting on the deck with their tops cut open with an axe and many Kodak flash cubes left by the insurance adjuster were everywhere.

The two guys that tried to burn her were nowhere to be found. They hid out in the middle of Prince William Sound for an entire month pretending to hunt deer until the insurance adjuster left town.

Someone said that Jim Poor had my crab block so I walked over to his floating processing ferry barge, went into his office and said, "I want to borrow your pickup to get my crab block." I had never met Jim Poor before and he didn't know me but without batting an eye or saying a word he handed me the keys to his new truck.

I was young and strong in those days. I picked up the heavy crab block and carried it down the ramp to the float and hooked it back up to the davit on the side of the boat and connected the hydraulic hoses.

I needed a deckhand to help me get the boat cleaned up and underway. All the crews were busy fishing salmon and the only one person I could find was Jose who couldn't speak any English. Jose was desperate to find work. I paid him $8 an hour which was more than minimum wage at the time. I don't know if he was an illegal alien and I didn't care. All I could get out of him was he was mad at the federally because they had shot him in the leg and raped his girlfriend. His whole goal in life was to make enough money to buy a machine gun and go back to Mexico to kill federally.

We had a difficult time communicating but as luck would have it Jose was a trained Cummings diesel mechanic. Cummings had a large engine manufacturing plant in Mexico. Jose understood more about diesel engines that I did. Sometimes you got to wonder if there is some unseen hand of providence guiding our paths through life.

We wrapped towels over our mouths and scraped most of the charcoal in the engine room and painted everything white. We cleaned the dry chemical fire extinguisher powder off the engine and I used house wiring and a row of knife switches to hook up the bilge pumps. I installed three large 12-volt truck batteries and ordered a 36-volt alternator from Anchorage.

The Bank of Cordova was very friendly. Apparently my name was famous because many decades prior my father brought three live wolverines into town and sold them to Dock Chase for $900 apiece. The bank gave me a desk and a phone to use any time I needed one. My father's reputation had preceded me. The Mad Trapper was also a famous pilot and a friend of Bob Reeve. I had money to fix up the Mary M and the bank was hoping I would do business with them in the future.

We were almost ready to start the engine when I noticed a three-inch diameter washer lying on top of the number one cylinder. Each cylinder has individual rocker-arm shafts. The shaft had broken because some idiot set the valve clearance wrong. This allowed the spacer washer to fall on top of the cylinder head. Each cylinder has three rocker arms. The shafts have a ¼-inch offset in the middle so that then rotated ¼ of a turn it lowers the middle rocker arm down on the little start valve allowing compressed air into the cylinder to push the piston down to start the engine.

I removed the broken 2 1/4-inch by 18-inch long shaft and took the pieces over to Jim Poor's cannery. It turned out that the machinist and hot-headed, cannery-boss was Christen Anderson who I had met at the Snug Harbor cannery on Chisik Island several years before. He looked at the shaft and shook his head saying, "I can't help you because I am way to busy right now with the salmon coming in." "This job will take many hours." Finally he said, "Theirs a fisherman I know who has a lathe in his garage." He gave me a piece of shafting and told me how to make an offset center to turn the shaft down.

I walked a mile or so up the hill to the fisherman's garage. Fortunately the fisherman was home and he graciously allowed me to use his metal lathe free of charge while he went fishing. I offered him money but he refused. By then it was late afternoon. I centered each end of the shaft slightly more than 1/4-inch off center, drilled a center hole and gnawed away on it all night. When an offset is chucked between live centers the shaft flops up and down. After a few hours of staring at it can make you sick. I nibbled away on end of the shaft over eight hours until it had two four-inch by 2-inch diameter shaft on each end to slide the rocker arms on. This left, a 4-inch by ¼-inch offset in the middle to depress the air valve. By eight the next morning I staggered down to the boat and handed the new shaft to my Mexican, Cummings-trained, engineer and went to bed.

I awoke at noon to discover that the ends of the shaft were a couple thousands of an inch too large to allow the rocker arms to slip on. Jose had taken the new part down to Mr. Chris Anderson. He was so impressed by what I had accomplished overnight that he chucked it in his lathe and removed enough metal to allow the rocker arms to slip on. You could say that I was lucky but sometimes you got to wonder if there is something more than luck taking place.

Finally, I was ready to start the engine. I rolled the flywheel over with an iron bar to the start position, pumped up 200 pounds per square inch of air pressure with the Lister auxiliary, pumped up the fuel pressure with the hand lever and pulled the start lever. It rolled over and started with a loud clank and kept running. The steel oil tank mounted on the bulkhead aft of the engine bulged out like a balloon under pressure and oil was squirting out of the plastic vent hose because the fire had melted shut. What I didn't know, was Atlas engines have a dry sump. A piston pumps forces oil into all the bearings and as the oil leaks down into the sump it is pumped back up by another piston pump into the oil reservoir tank. The Atlas kept running and running and I didn't know how to shut it off. I closed every fuel valve and it kept running and running.

Later on I asked a guy who was familiar with old diesel engines how to stop them. He said, "Oh you just pull out on the rack." At the time I didn't know what the rack was so I had to ask him. Under each push rod that opens the injectors at the top of the cylinder is a metal wedge. The wedges are connected to a lever that connects to a 1-inch shaft that connects to a fly-ball, governor. The shaft connecting all the wedges together is called the rack.

The next day I started the engine and attempted to move the boat over to the fuel dock. The bow carried of three piling cabled together at the top. I am sure that at least two of them broke underwater. It took me a while to get the hang of handling such a large vessel.

Ten days after arriving in Cordova we finally got underway. Many of the locals said the boat would never move again, but we did it. It was a beautiful day and the weather was flat calm. I steered the boat from high up on the flying bridge. Suddenly I noticed the oil pressure gage registered zero. It had been hanging at three pounds per square inch earlier and about six pounds per square inch down in the engine room. I ran down and stopped the engine and looked for the cause of why there was no oil pressure. I started her up again--still no oil pressure. I stopped her again. Finally I noticed that a one-inch pin had worked its way out of the yoke on the piston pump. I pushed it back where it belonged and inserted a 16-penny nail for a cotter pin to keep it in place.

I was intent on going non-stop all the way to Seldovia. I was a lot younger and tougher in those days and was used to staying up two or three days at a time. We were abeam of Ellrington Island when I saw salmon spilling out of the bow wake. I couldn't believe my eyes. The boat was running through a giant school of fish. A good twenty minutes passed while live salmon tumbling out of the bow wake. Suddenly there were seals and purposes everywhere. I was so amazing that I turned the boat around, ran back thru the fish and got everyone up to watch so that they wouldn't think I was crazy.

After resting up for a day in Seldovia I had noticed one of the cylinders was knocking. I removed the 18-inch diameter manholes on the lower port side of the block and peered inside. One of the rod bearing caps appeared to be loose and flopping up and down each time that cylinder fired. I inserted a chunk of solder under the bearing cap and tightened the bolts. I removing the mashed solder and using a micrometer measured its thickness. The book called for a rod-bearing clearance of eight to ten-thousandths of an inch. The rod bearing clearance was over twelve thousandths so I filed a little metal off the bearing cap with a flat file where it meets up with the piston rod thereby reducing the clearance to nine thousandths. I tightened the rod bolts thinking to myself "That'll work fine for a few years."

We fished salmon in Tuxedni Bay that summer and I paid Jose live on the Mary M and grind the valves on the Atlas. The valves are in cages sealed with copper gaskets. I annealed all the copper gaskets to make them soft and Jose hand lapped the valve seats with valve grinding compound.

New boats entering the fishery at the time were not greeted with much adulation. I had difficulty selling my crab in Seldovia because the plant managers were threatened.

That first year I had discovered a small school of crab ten to twelve miles off Augustine volcano and managed to catch about 36,000 pounds. At fifty cents a pound that amounted to only $15,000. Not too bad for two weeks fishing. By that time Jose had made enough money to buy his machine gun and go back to Mexico to kill federally so he was anxious to leave.

A year later I was heading toward Augustine Island at night when a larger vessel headed toward us on a collision course. We were about fifteen miles west of Seldovia. To keep from colliding with the other vessel I turned the wheel hard right. The eighty-six-foot power scow kept turning toward us. It had a big steel bow and appeared to be the Widgeon Two. It was now following us about 200 feet off our stern and kept following as the Mary M turned in a big 360-degree circle. It was trying to hit us! They were getting closer because the Mary M's bottom was fouled with a thick layer of barnacles. I pulled the throttle levers up all the way up and we held our distance. After making a couple 360-degree turns I took out my 30-caliber army rifle and bounced a few bullets off their big steel bow. If they refused to veer off I was prepared to spray their wheel house windows with bullets. Fortunately, after hearing the shots they veer off and headed toward Homer.

After that near collision I turned the boat around and headed back to Seldovia to put the Mary M on the grid. Using wood boards with 1/8th inch metal scrapers attached my crew and I removed the heavy coating of barnacles and marine growth. Later I talked about the incident to Mr. Gregwire, manager of Alaska Seafood in Homer. He said, "Damn, he could have sunk both boats."

After fishing king crab with Mary M three years I ran her south to Anacortes, Washington and put her in Tony Loverick's shipyard. The yard owner and his family were from Yugoslavia and had owned a ship yard capable of hauling a 5000 ton ships before Hitler took over his yard with World War Two. The family had to leave their business. After fighting in the French Underground Tony moved to America and started over. Tony was also a hard hat diver and salver. He had raised two very large barges to use as breakwaters in from of his marine railway.

We spent almost three months in the shipyard replacing 32 planks and a new bow stem, forefoot and false keel damage from when it went on the rocks in Raspberry Strait. I had the old bow iron galvanized at Scots Galvanizing in Ballard and bought a large piece of gumwood for the new stem. The yard cut all the timbers including the gumwood with their giant band saws.

We traveled though the Locks to Lake Union and made our way to Eastlake where Columbia Wards had a dock and boat storage for their fleet of tenders. The lock bosses like to yell at young guys with big boats and try to humiliate them; pretending they don't know how to tie up a boat. In reality they are bored with their meaningless civil service job and only do it for amusement.

My single crewman at the time was Jerry Welch from New York State. Jerry was my best friend and the best pool player I ever met. He had helped me remove the 20,000 pound Atlas Imperial at Columbia Wards cannery dock at Eastlake in Seattle and install the rebuilt Caterpillar engine that Joe Fribrock had located for me. I couldn't have rebuilt the Mary M without help from several friends.

Jerry and I each had two pair of coveralls to protect our clothing when working on the engines. Using cum-a-longs we unbolted the fifty-year-old engine parts and drug aft through a passageway cut through a bulkhead into the fish hold we got quite greasy. At noon we broke for lunch and carefully peeled our greasy coveralls off with two fingers into a black garbage bag. After lunch we put on our clean coveralls and went back to work. At five we peeled the second pair off and hiked up the launder mat. We put our four pair of coveralls in two machines dumped in a bunch of Tide soap. They were so greasy that they came out of the wash feeling oily. They were still so greasy that they probably would have kept you dry in a rainstorm. While walking out the door of the launder mat we were frequently amused by the screams of a woman who had put her fine underwear into one of the machines we had used to wash out coveralls.

On weekends we played pool in one of the beer joints up the hill. One had ten pool tables. Jerry usually managed to make twenty dollars or so before we left. That was our daily routine. Eventually we got the Cat installed, the 32-volt jog steering system and a hundred other details taken care of. It was time to test out the new Mary M. It was the most wonderful feeling I have ever experienced cruising at top speed on Lake Washington in front of Bill Gate's house. The Caterpillar diesel was so quiet that engine noise was drowned out by the bow wake.

We departed Seattle the spring of 1975 and headed north up through the Straits of Georgia through Canada. We didn't bother checking with customs in those days. We just went wherever we wanted to go. I had trouble with the air starter on the new Cat so I pulled into the little Canadian village, Clem Too. The plastic veins in the starter housing broke some of the case iron air vents.

I am one of those guys who can fix just about anything. I filled the broken cast iron holes with Marine Tex. As for the Bakelite veins

I noticed that the thickness of the veins was about the same thickness as the Masonite clipboard in the wheelhouse. I carefully cut new veins off the clipboard, sanded tem down and put the starter back together. It worked great and we got underway after doing a little shopping in Canada.

A day later we stopped in Ketchikan to fuel up and fill the new fresh water tank. By that time the twenty new crab pots I had lashed to the back deck were starting to move from side to side so I tack welded them to the metal strips on the makeshift crab rack.

Three days later we stopped at Yakutat to visit the Mayor, Byron Mallott and his family. I decided to leave the next day before the weather changed. Byron would later become Alaska's lieutenant Governor in 2016.

I don't like to write about what happened next because it was so terrifying and the fact that I was afraid for my wife and kids who were onboard. The weather forecast wasn't great. The forecast was southeast 25 increasing to 30 knots. We didn't want to hang around Yakutat for four or five more days waiting for weather so I decided to leave. Since the weather would be on the stern I figured we would have a good ride up to Prince William Sound and be inside in about 30 hours.

As it turned out we got caught in the storm of a century. Boats and planes went down all over Alaska. After departing Yakutat the wind freshened as predicted. By the time we passed Kayak Island it was blowing forty. The autopilot I had rigged to the jog station worked perfectly keeping the bow pointing directly away from the giant swells. I felt sorry for my wife, Pat my four kids huddled in the galley.

Earlier I clamped a half pot of beans on the stove so after traveling twelve hours we had something to eat. By that time it was blowing eighty. When down in the trough you could not see the tops of the ocean swells. Each wave filled the back deck almost to the tops of the twenty six by six pots that I had welded to the deck in Ketchikan. Then the Mary M shuddered from side to side as the stern rose up and the giant waves passed under us. I was amazed as the powerful Cat engine lugged down and we slid backwards down the back side of the waves fifteen feet or so. Eventually we rose to the top of the wave. It was quite terrifying to look down the almost vertical ten stories as we were catapulted forward twenty knots down the giant swells. We were actually surfing a 72-foot boat and in grave danger of broaching sideways. If a boat broaches, it can roll the boat completely upside down as happened with so many boats in the past. Fortunately my makeshift autopilot held a true directly away from the giant swells.

Thirty miles from Hinchinbrook Island and the entrance of Prince William Sound and safety the swells abated and the wind switched around from southeast to northeast. Ten miles from Hinchinbrook entrance the wind picked up to fifty or so knots with sixteen-foot swells directly on the bow. My old radar had a limited range of only twelve miles so I wasn't too sure if we were going directly in the entrance of Prince William Sound or heading to the rock pile south of the entrance.

After what we had been through, bucking twelve to sixteen-foot waves seemed tame so I failed to cut back on the throttle. The trouble with sixteen-foot waves was they were only twenty-feet apart. The Mary M rose up and dived deep into an oncoming swell. All the wheelhouse windows were underwater taking out two plate glass windows. I ducked the flying glass but a large amount of water came pouring in with much force. All the electronics in the wheelhouse ceased to function and with no radar, no radios and no autopilot meant that I had to steer into the weather using only the magnetic compass. I pulled back on the throttle and the boat rode comfortably like a duck on the water. I told Jerry to take the wheel.

When the wave came through the windows a foot high wave of water and plate glass ran through the passage way back into the galley. I heard my wife and kids scream. I saw the galley had with a foot of seawater sloshing back and forth. I knew it would drain down through holes in the floor in a few minutes so I knew my family would be safe. I assured them that we were not sinking and that everything would be just fine and that we would be inside Prince William Sound very soon. My kids looked up at me with terrified eyes shivering as seawater sloshed around their feet.

I ran back to the wheel house and grabbed the wheel away from Jerry. The wind was whistling through the broken windows but no spray was coming in. I told Jerry to get a hammer and nails along with all the board he could fine. I handed him and old raincoat and told him to nail it over the windows and put some boards on to hold it in place. Later he reported that the wind was blowing so hard that he had to swing the hammer six-inches to one side of the nail in order to hit it. He also said that due to the cold he had hit his thumb and didn't even feel it. All this took place in the month of April and there was still snow on the mountains and glaciers of Prince William Sound.

After Jerry was back inside I eased the throttle forward land became visible through the mist. We slowly crept forward leaping over a fifteen-foot-high chop into the sound. Once inside I thought it would calm down but it was quite rough. It was like a good rough day on Cook Inlet. We crawled across the sound toward a bay with the name Snug Harbor on the charts. We anchored up for a day before heading toward Seward, Seldovia and our home in Halibut Cove. After arriving in Seldovia we discovered the devastation the super storm had made all over Alaska. Boats and planes had gone down everywhere. I lost a good friend who crashed his 206 Cessna while taking off in Jakaloff Bay. If we had been killed you wouldn't be reading this.

CHAPTER SIX

Billion-Dollars A Year Stolen From The Private Sector

by Henry Kroll

There has been a covert war against the private sector to quash opposition to selling oil leases in lower Cook Inlet. This state allowed the destruction of a billion dollar a year renewable resource fishery in favor of a non-renewable resource. We Alaskans are tired of being ripped off and forced into poverty.

From 1960 to 2000 this state allowed two oil tankers a day to each dumped six to ten-million gallons of ballast water taken from Los Angeles, Honolulu, Anacortes, and Korean and other boat harbors. Oil tankers have to take on ballast water to run in the open ocean otherwise they will flip over. According to reference on this they take on 140,000 to 400,000 barrels of water. That's amounts to 180-million gallons. The contaminated water they brought to Alaska contained trillions of bacteria, algae and nematodes that eat the inside out of the shrimp and crab eggs. You got to do the math to understand how this is possible. Sixty-five billion gallons of contaminated tanker ballast water each year for thirty years plus drill tailings from 200 oil wells, plus oil from military vessels and cruise ships destroyed a billion dollar a year shrimp and crab resource. The state statute fine for dumping ballast water was $500.

ABOUT ME

I fished king crab twenty-five years. I built a house and shop in Halibut Cove. We lost everything due to State greed. We were forced to move onto our salmon fish sites in Tuxedni Bay. Our children suffered because we were destitute. Hundreds of fishermen lost their boats and gear worth a billion dollars.

The fishery is supposed to be a renewable resource but when you got a state intent on raking in Billions from the sale of oil leases the private sector hasn't got a chance. They wanted to make Cook Inlet look like the Gulf of Mexico with oil rigs all the way down Shelikoff Strait. The State never sold many oil leases in lower Cook Inlet because apparently there is little oil there. This terrible crime and violation of the state constitution for the destruction of the crab and shrimp resources was for nothing. It was a crime borrowed from the federal government's COLD WAR covert-operations of social engineering and mind control.

It wasn't always fun and games out off Augustine Island volcano in the winter:

3   12 76

3   11 76

I ran the Mary M south to Seattle two different winters and borrowed money from Seattle First bank to install 32 new planks, new forefoot and bow stem. I also installed a new D-342 D-8 Caterpillar engine. The Mary M was one of the fastest boats in the fleet.

She looked great when we left the shipyard in Anacortes. Her draft was 9 feet.

Me removing the Atlas and installing the D-342 Caterpillar Diesel.

Below is a picture of the remaining two cylinders as I was removing it from the Mary M.

Below picture of my boat Mary M and the house I built in Halibut Cove. We lost everything after the crab and shrimp resources were destroyed by foreign bacteria and algae.

It took me many years to figure out what happened to the crab resource. At the time, 40-years ago, we didn't know what was happening to us. Thousands of cannery workers lost their jobs and many processors went bankrupt. Several towns lost their infrastructure and had to depend on State and Federal grants to provide services to their residents. Conservatively speaking, the total cost to the private sector is over billion dollars a year.

Over a 50 year time period the State of Alaska turned a blind eye to the dumping of billions of gallons of oil tanker ballast water into lower Cook Inlet taken from the Los Angeles, Honolulu and Anacortes boat harbors – the primary cause of the demise of the crab and shrimp fisheries in Kodiak and lower Cook Inlet.

Between 1960 to 1990 the State of Alaska also ignored leaking underwater pipelines and the dumping of drill tailings from over 200 wells and "eight" major oil well blowouts that mixed billions of gallons of oil and natural gas into the tide waters. The tremendous amount of toxins released into the environment reduced the biomass of the plankton blooms and altered the organisms that make up the food chain thus causing the decimation of the shrimp and crab fisheries in Cook Inlet and Kodiak.

After the crab disappeared the processing plants went bankrupt and forced to close hundreds of people who worked in the fish plants lost their jobs and had to relocate. Hundreds of fishermen including myself lost our boats and gear totaling over a billion dollars. It was not only a Constitutional Violation it was a betrayal of public trust and a crime of gigantic proportions.

My boat Mary M and crew.

This was one of my first catches of king crab. Ron Bales is overseeing the catch.

Greg Prescott untying the pot.

My best season was a catch of 196,000 pounds of king crab in three weeks. We'd quit fishing my salmon set-nets to fish 16-miles off Augustine Volcano starting August 10 to September 1st every year for ten years. When crab catches dwindled due to foreign bacteria, algae and nematodes I was forced to travel to Kodiak and further west to King Cove.

We also had a winter season in January where we fished king crab and tanners (snow crab) in the middle of Kachemak Bay south of Homer. I also used to catch 100,000 pounds of tanner crab commencing November 15 to the end of February in Kachemak Bay.

When the Cook Inlet king crab and tanners disappeared I fished out of Kukak Bay five seasons. Kukak Bay is located south of Cape Douglass thirty miles. The season started February 15 to the end of March and I usually caught more than 200,000 pounds. The number of tanners dwindled but was still fishable in that location when the Alaska Department of Fish and game closed the tanner season permanently.

It wasn't always fun and games. If the wind wasn't blowing Augustine volcano erupted coating us with volcanic ash. My tanner pots came up with pumas on them and we had to shovel it back overboard.

Twenty-million-gallons of sewage discharged daily from the City of Anchorage and more from Palmer and Wasilla outflows contribute to the ongoing environmental damage robbing crab and shrimp fishermen of approximately a $500,000,000.00 annual resource harvest. Double that for the value added product to the processors and towns equals over a billion dollars a year.

Me above. Below the Homer Harbor.

Below we are tied to Columbia Ward's dock in Lake Union Seattle.

Mary M in Port Townsend, Washington.

FINES FOR DUMPING TANKER AND SHIP BALLAST WATER – ALASKA STATUTES

§ 30.25.010   ALASKA STATUTES SUPPLEMENT   § 30.50.020

Secs. 30.25.010 — 30.25.360. Policy; regulation of facilities and marine carriers; certificates of risk avoidance; emergencies; removal of prohibited discharges; enforcement; penalties; coastal protection fund.

Repealed by § 11 ch 116 SLA 1980.

Cross references. — For provisions concerning oil pollution control, see AS 46.04.010 — 46.04.120.

Editor's notes. — The repealed chapter derived from § 2, ch. 266, SLA 1976.

NOTES TO DECISIONS

Construction of chapter. — See Chevron U.S.A., Inc. v. Hammond (A77- 195 Civil), F. Supp. (D. Alas. 1978).

Chapter 50. Miscellaneous Provisions.

Section
10. Interfering with buoys and beacons
20. Discharging ballast into navigable waters

Sec. 30.50.010. Interfering with buoys and beacons. A person who moors a vessel, boat, skiff, barge, scow, raft, or part of a raft to a buoy or beacon placed in the navigable waters of the state, or in a bay, river, or arm of the sea bordering the state by the authority of the United States Coast Guard, or who hangs on with a vessel, boat, skiff, barge, scow, raft, or part of a raft to the buoy or beacon, or who wilfully removes, damages, or destroys the buoy or beacon, or who cuts down, removes, damages, or destroys a beacon erected on land in the state by authority of the United States Coast Guard is guilty of a misdemeanor, and upon conviction is punishable by a fine of not less than $100 nor more than $200, or by imprisonment in a jail for not less than one month nor more than six months, or by both. (§ 65-14-2 ACLA 1949; am § 22 ch 166 SLA 1978)

Revisor's notes. — The section is derived from the present AS 11.65.020 and was renumbered by the revisor of statutes pursuant to § 22, ch. 166, SLA 1978

(revision of the criminal code). Cross references. — As to sentences for misdemeanors, see AS 12.55.135.

Sec. 30.50.020. Discharging ballast into navigable waters. A person, whether or not he is an officer of a vessel, who discharges the ballast of a vessel into the navigable portion or channel of a bay, harbor, or river of the state, or within the jurisdiction of the state, so as to injuriously affect the navigable portion or channel, or to obstruct the navigation of the navigable portion or channel, upon conviction, is

202

- Note: I found this old book of Alaska Statutes in the Seldovia Dump 28 years ago. It looked important so I kept it. The fine mentioned on the document below is between $100 and $500 and between three months and a year in jail for dumping something that pollutes or obstructs a navigable river, bay or channel in the State of Alaska. If you want to know how it pertains to tanker ballast water I will have to take a trip to the Legislative Affairs office to look up cross reference AS 46.03.750 which I will have to do on Tuesday.

§ 30.50.020   NAVIGATION, HARBORS AND SHIPPING   § 30.50.020

punishable by imprisonment in a jail for not less than three months nor
more than one year, or by a fine of not less than $100 nor more than
$500. (§ 65-14-1 ACLA 1949; § 22 ch 166 SLA 1978)

Revisor's notes. — The section is   (revision of the criminal code).
derived from the present AS 11.65.010 and   **Cross references.** — As to ballast
was renumbered by the revisor of statutes   water discharge, see AS 46.03.750.
pursuant to § 22, ch. 166, SLA 1978

AS 46.03.750. Ballast Water Discharge.

(a) Except as provided in (b) of this section, a person may not cause
    or permit the discharge of ballast water from a cargo tank of
    a tank vessel into the waters of the state. A tank vessel may
    not take on petroleum or a petroleum product or by-product
    as cargo unless it arrives in ports in the state without having
    discharged ballast from cargo tanks into the waters of the state
    and the master of the vessel certifies that fact on forms provided
    by the department.

(b) The master of a tank vessel may discharge ballast water from a
    cargo tank of a tank vessel if it is necessary for the safety of the
    tank vessel and no alternative action is feasible to ensure the
    safety of the tank vessel.

**That's all well and good however what they don't tell you is 'at
the time there was heavy tanker traffic, 'state waters' only extend out
to three miles offshore'. Obviously large oil tankers cannot run close
to shore otherwise they might run aground and who is measuring
the distance? Where are the forms provided by what department?**

A STATE FUNDED MOVIE

In a state documentary titled, EXXON VALDEZE TWENTY
YEARS AFTER THE SPILL 'State biologists stated that they had
identified 300 foreign species that were introduced into Prince William

Sound from oil tanker ballast water.' How many species of foreign organisms were not identified? Three thousand?-- thirty thousand? How many foreign organisms like worms and nematodes that bore inside crab and shrimp eggs were introduced into Cook Inlet and Kodiak waters from 1960 to 2014?

I FISHED 16 MILES EAST OF AUGUSTINE VOLCANO OVER TEN YEARS.

Heading across 3/8/76

During the thirty years oil tankers were dumping ballast water from un-segregated ballast tanks into Cook Inlet, many more millions of gallons of crude oil was dumped into Cook Inlet than was spilled by the Exxon Valdez in 1989. Un-segregated ballast tanks still had many thousands of gallons of crude oil in the bottom when they take on the ballast water. Pumps lose their prime after sucking up twenty feet leaving a foot or more of crude in the bottom of the tanks.

The fact that there was oil in the ballast water is the least of the crime. It's the foreign bacteria, algae and nematodes in the water that alter the plankton blooms and eat the crab and shrimp eggs. Some algae can multiply up to 2-times every 12 hours. Some bacteria divide every four hours. When there are no predators, algae and bacteria they can replace the natural plankton blooms in ten years killing off all the clams, king crab, tanner crab, Dungeness crab and everything else that spawns in the shallow water.

Algae are like the old riddle "Would you rather have a million dollars or a penny that doubles every day for a year?" One tiny foreign algae with no predictors growing in oxygen rich waters with lots of food can alter the food chain. When you have trillions of them in 20-million gallons of ballast water from one oil tanker you have a recipe for disaster.

The late 1970's were tough:

I had invested over $200,000.00 in a 128-foot processing ship Orion located in Seattle. America was experiencing a depression. Cars were lined up at the gas pumps waiting to get gas and banks were closing all over the country. You couldn't borrow money if you were god.

I borrowed $50,000 from First Interstate bank before they went under to pay my crew who had been working on the Orion. After the crab disappeared there was no way to make money without our boats. Halibut was selling for 12 cents a pound due to a mercury scare.

The bank adjusting officer came after me putting a Marshal sticker on the Mary M. I tried negotiating with him and continued to fish crab. I had to keep going further west out the Aleutian Chain to fish king crab eventually fishing out of King Cove.

The spring of 1980 I experienced a divorce and lost both the Mary M and the Orion. I made an agreement with the bank to fished the last Kodiak king crab season and broke even. During my divorce in 1980 Judge Hansen berated me from the bench indicating that he hated my guts. He had tried commercial fishing and wasn't very successful so there may have been some kind of personal animosity involved.

The strain of losing everything I had poured my life blood into caused me to have a stroke. I remember the day in Seattle at my mother's house when noticed I couldn't speak. I wanted to speak but the words wouldn't come out of my mouth. My inability to articulate words from the stroke lasted about 25-years and sometimes I still can't formulate complete sentences.

I re-married in 1983 to a nice lady from Seattle who wanted to get out of Seattle. I still had trouble speaking. At the present time we have been married 35-years.

In 1988 I was sued over a skiff collision and couldn't testify in court because I couldn't speak complete sentences. Judge Hansen presided over the case saying that I had to pay Plaintiff $28,000. Judge Hansen sat on the case four years and died of brain cancer.

My wife, Mary and I fished our salmon sites and I made the last $26,000 land payment to the State of Alaska for the homestead in 1995. That was a big mistake because once the land was paid off free and clear the crooked lawyers invaded the Kroll Children Trust and took our land.

After that, Judge Cranston took over and sat on the case another three years. He kept ordering me to attend hearings. By that time I was really tired of this lawsuit and couldn't attend the last hearing in Kenai because I didn't have any money to travel. When I didn't show up Judge Cranston ruled in favor of the Plaintiff giving him our homestead land and home in Tuxedni Bay. One year later Judge Cranston was accused of molesting Boy Scouts and died of a heart attack.

We lost the homestead land after putting I had put it into an irrevocable trust for my children to comply with Judge Hansen's Divorce Decree. My Attorney Allan Beiswenger didn't even know who owned the homestead land. That's how stupid he was. It seems I always wind up with the dumbest lawyers on the planet.

Liberals don't like people who earn the original dollar. Original dollars are earned when you do actual work. You harvest what God or Mother Nature provides. You dig a clam and sell it to get original dollars to feed our family or you cut down a tree to build a canoe and sell it to get original dollars to feed your family. Here in Alaska the alleged state operating in fraud claims all the resources. You can't dig a clam or cut down a tree paying some parasite.

The real crime here is the fact that we were evicted out of their home by Judge William Morse for no reason thus stopping us from teaching our twelve grandchildren boat handling, wilderness

living skills and how to our salmon set-net sites. This bogus lawsuit interfered and altered the lives of over twenty members of my family causing them to suffer pain and hardship far into the future. This occurred after Judge Morse ruled that we could no longer live in our home on the sand spit and venture onto our Federal homestead land where we had poured our life blood to prove up on for the Feds and constructed homes and then had to buy it back from the state.

The real crime is the lack of our bush lifestyle where we can teach our children and grandchildren the many skills like boat handling we could have taught them. Their future and ours could have been much richer and happier if we had honest Judges and penny pinching lawyers who will do anything for money.

My free market capitalist ideas classed with Tony Knowles war on small business and commercial fishermen. Tony Knowles stated several times that he disliked commercial fishermen. Tony Knowles is the Governor who appointed William Morse to be the Superior Court Judge in 2002. He is the judge who ruled in favor of Governor Knowles confiscation of half your dividend check last year.

Tony Knowles also gave our state halibut and cod resource management away to the Feds--a clear violation of the State Constitution and Treason. There was no need to do this because Alaska already had its enforcement officers in place. Now we have one or more federal officers in every port in Alaska poking their noses into fish holds and inspecting licenses. Food is a weapon and Federal control of any food can be used against citizens to punish them and put down any revolution against government tyranny and oppression.

I believe he gave our fishery away to the Feds in the hope they would make him vice President of the United States under Bush. I say this because Tony Knowles attend Yale University and was a fellow Bones-man along with George Bush, Al Gore and Bill Clinton. The Skull and Bones Fraternity controlled by the superrich grooms it members to control the future directions of this country. Much like the Masons they grant special favors to its members like getting high paying government jobs as long as they obey their masters and the secret oaths they took that supersede all oaths they might take in the future. This is how our government works!

> Our State Constitution demands that Alaskans come first. As a native born Alaska born in the territory of Alaska 75-years ago in Seldovia, Alaska I demand that all State Agents obey the oaths they were sworn to uphold—particularly Article Eight. *"Nowadays common sense is an endangered species."* --Native Leader, Steven Hunnington

Public officials coming to Alaska from New York, Peoria, Illinois and other places to find jobs are unfamiliar with the Culture and the knowledge necessary to make a living in Bush Alaska. Although Native Alaskans have been living in harmony with the environment for a couple thousand years they think the people who live in Alaska are primitive and stupid and incapable of managing our own affairs. I know for a fact that most of them don't have the guts and fortitude to make a living commercial fishing or trapping yet they think they are smarter than the native Alaskans and must tell Native Alaskans how they should live their lives.

Public officials and government psychiatrists can never figure out the root of the problem of why there are so many Native Alaskan's on the streets and in jail. The only solution they can come up with to fix the problem is to build more prisons, and hire more prosecutors and Judges. Most believe that all money must come from the government. They don't know what original dollars are.

The Department of Corrections figures: as of December 1, 2012, list the number of Alaska Native Alaskans in prison compared with other races in Alaska as 66.08 % statewide. Over half the prison populations are native Alaskans. The 2010 census lists Alaska's total Native population as 14.8 percent. It's all about "charging" them with something to take their land and birth bonds. The Judges and Prosecutors get a percentage of the many millions of dollars taken. The Department of Corrections gets to keep a portion of their Permanent Fund dividend checks. Public policy is about money.

The number of <u>Alaska Native women</u> in Alaska's prisons is 75.94 percent compared with other races yet the total native population is only 14.8%.. Do you see the disparity here? Did Native women write the laws? Did Native men and women write the State Constitution? Other occupied nations around the world don't lock up so many of their indigenous populations. Why are so many native women being sterilized?

Alaska has a higher demographic percentage of indigenous populations in prison than any other nation in the world. Alaska is a military occupation state.

CHAPTER SEVEN

Additional Pollution

There were eight oil well blowouts between 1960 and the year 2000. In 1983 the Grayling Platform blew natural gas and some oil 1,200 feet into the air for one week and settled down to about 500-feet above the rig for one month before they could get divers down there to shut it off. I estimate that it released more gas into the atmosphere than all the gas that was liquefied and sold in the Nikiski plant.

REGIONAL CITIZEN'S ADVISORY COUNCIL (RCAC) Invasive species in ballast water.

Why do tankers use ballast water?

After offloading the crude oil cargo tanks at a refinery, empty oil tankers take on ballast water to ensure vessel trim and stability during ocean voyages. Prior to loading their cargo, the tankers must discharge the ballast water used during the voyage. Crude oil is loaded onto empty tankers at the Valdez Marine Terminal (VMT). Segregated ballast water is discharged directly into Port Valdez.

The Grayling Platform blowout of May 23, 1985 blew natural gas, oil and tide water 1,200 feet into the air for one week then subsided down to 500-feet above the rig tower for one entire month. I estimate that it wasted more natural gas than was ever sold and shipped out of Alaska.

How much oil was mixed with the gas is anybody's guess. According to the Coast Guard there was some oil.

The Steelhead Platform caught fire in Cook Inlet off Nikiski December 21, 1987.

Tankers can carry 150,000-400,000 barrels of ballast water per trip. That is 6.3-million to 16-million gallons+ for each tanker. ---RCAC (Regional Citizens Advisory Council)

How much ballast water comes to Valdez?

Tankers can carry 150,000-400,000 barrels **(6.3-million gallons to 16.8-million gallons)** of ballast water per trip. A barrel of crude is 42 gallons. *[My estimates of 10-million gallons per tanker entering Cook Inlet were too low.]* As of 2006, tankers arrived in Valdez approximately 312 times each year to offload ballast water and load crude oil. Until 1998, tankers arrived about 700 times annually. The number of tanker arrivals has been slowly declining due to the decreased output of crude oil from the North Slope oil fields. Estimates for 1998 alone put the number of gallons of segregated ballast water discharged into Prince William Sound at 107 million. ---RCAC

What is the difference between segregated and unsegregated ballast water?

Crude oil tankers that serve the VMT either fill "empty" crude oil tanks with ballast water or fill dedicated ballast water tanks with water for the return trip to Valdez. When an empty crude oil tank is filled with ballast water, that water is typically referred to as "unsegregated" or "dirty" ballast because the ballast uses the same tanks as the crude oil rather than a separate tank. Although every effort is made at the refinery to completely unload the oil from the cargo tanks prior to loading the tanks with ballast water, some residual oil inevitably remains on the tank walls and floor and mixes with the ballast water, creating an oily water mixture that requires treatment prior to discharge into the ocean. Most new tankers are designed with segregated ballast tanks, but a few older tankers that service the Valdez terminal are only able to carry unsegregated ballast. ---RCAC

Studies completed on unsegregated oily ballast water at the VMT have shown that the amounts of hydrocarbons in the oily ballast water are lethal to aquatic or benthic species in the ballast tanks. Based on this research, it is unlikely that non-indigenous species in unsegregated ballast water would survive the trip. As a result, unsegregated ballast has been eliminated from the PWSRCAC NIS project scope of concern, and the project's emphasis has concentrated on the control and treatment of segregated ballast water. ---RCAC

Where is the ballast water from?

Approximately 86% of the ballast water discharged into Port Valdez originates from the ports of Puget Sound, San Francisco, and Long Beach. The residence time of segregated ballast water shipped from those ports is typically 5-10 days. This short residence time favors the survival of transported non-indigenous aquatic organisms in ballast water. Repeat inoculation of competent organisms on a high volume basis poses a serious NIS risk for the waters of Prince William Sound. Currently, no crude oil is being shipped to foreign ports from Alaska. ---RCAC

2003–Today

Although the foreign export of Alaska North Slope crude oil is still permitted by law, since 2003 the oil tankers from the Valdez Marine Terminal have been exporting only to domestic ports. The most common trade routes for oil tankers leaving Port Valdez are to refineries in:

- Puget Sound, Washington: Anacortes, Cherry Point, Ferndale, Port Angeles, Tacoma
- San Francisco Bay, California: Benicia, Martinez, Richmond
- Southern California: El Segundo, LA/Long Beach

A limited number of shipments have also been made to refineries in Cook Inlet, Alaska (Nikiski) and Hawaii (Barber's Point). ---RCAC

1996-2002

In May 1996, a previous ban on export of crude oil from the Valdez Marine Terminal to foreign ports was lifted by Presidential order.

Shipment of oil to foreign ports increased the risk of non-indigenous aquatic species being transported back to Prince William Sound in tanker ballast water. ---RCAC

During 1996-2002 the majority of the crude oil (about 95%) continued to be shipped to U.S. refineries; however, some crude oil (5% or less) was shipped to Japan, China, Korea, and Taiwan. ---RCAC

The Presidential order requires exporting tankers to adopt a mandatory program of deep water ballast exchange in at least 2,000 meters water depth. Exceptions to this requirement can be made by the tanker captain to ensure the safety of the vessel and crew. Record keeping requirements are in place to document that deep water ballast exchange is being conducted. (15 CFR 754.2). Tankers sailing to domestic ports are not required to practice deep water ballast exchange. ---RCAC

1977-1996 The Valdez Marine Terminal and the Trans-Alaska Pipeline System began operations in 1977. Between 1977 and 1996, 11 billion barrels of oil were shipped from Port Valdez to refineries in U.S. ports. (Prior 1996, U.S. law prohibited the export of crude oil from the Valdez Marine Terminal to foreign ports, with one exception to the Caribbean.) Not Honolulu Hawaii.

No ballast water treatment or management plan (including ballast exchange) was required during this time period. ---RCAC

In 1994 the Environmental Protection Agency ruled that Cook Inlet was a full flushing body of water and allowed oil drilling rigs to dump their drill tailings into Cook Inlet. Drill tailings from oil wells are radioactive containing radium 33 and radon gas. After they started dumping drill tailings the beluga whale population crashed. There used to be beluga whales swimming into the Kasioff and Kenai Rivers and now there are none. ---RCAC (Regional Citizens Advisory Council)

Pumps used to unload oil and ballast water aren't able to suck the tanks completely dry. They lose suction when there down to about 6-inches of oil. This means that there has to be at least six inches of crude or diesel left in the tanks when they pump water in from a foreign port. In addition, there would be tar balls stuck on the bulkheads and baffles inside the tank. As a result we lost a billion dollars a year crab and shrimp fishery that went into the privates sectors of Kodiak and Cook Inlet.

Liberals don't like people who earn the original dollar. Original dollars are earned when you do actual work. You harvest what God or Mother Nature provides. You dig a clam and sell it to get original dollars to feed our family or you cut down a tree to build a canoe and sell it to get original dollars to feed your family. Here in Alaska the alleged state operating in fraud claims all the resources. You can't dig a clam or cut down a tree paying some government parasite sitting behind a desk that is physically incapable of earning original dollars and who has never done an honest days' work in their life for a permit to dig that clam or cut down that tree. Does this alleged State Corporation incorporated in the State of Delaware really own anything?

Good left-wing Democrat will worship the Deep State and tow the party line. They deify public officials never questioning government adhering strictly to state policy…

If you want to have free will it is your duty as a citizen is to question government. You either question government or become a slave. We have seen what they do to people who don't question government during World War II in Nazi Germany.

THE LOSS OF THE CLAMS THAT LOCAL PEROPLE DEPENDED ON FOR FOOD IS MORE EVIDENCE OF POLLUTION INTRUDUCED BY THOUSANDS OF OIL TANKERS OVER A PERIOD OF THIRTY YEARS, LEAKY OIL PIPELINES AND WELL BLWOUTS. FOOD IS A WEAPON USED AGAINST ENEMY COMBATANTS. (US)

In addition to the crab fishery we also lost the clam resource due to greed and lust for big money for selling oil leases. The clams not only fed us they provided s source of income for some people. The first canneries constructed in Saldovia were built to can clams.

We used to have big, white hard-shell clams as big as your fist all up and down Seldovia Bay. You could dig just about anywhere a whole the size of a five-gallon bucket and fill up half a bucket of these very tasty clams. You didn't want to dig near town because of the sewage draining into the slough but anywhere across the bay or outside the little island in front of the bay you could get all the clams you want on a run-out tide. The beaches were alive. Worms of all sorts lived in the mud and creatures of all sorts scurried around in the hole you dug. Green seaweed and bladder kelp covered he rocks. Snails and limpid lived in and under the seaweed.

When you looked down the beach into the sun it looked like a sprinkler system going off because the clams squirted water up to four feet into the air. When you walked down the beach with hip boots on I kid you not, your pants would get wet from the clams squirting on them.

After the state allowed two oil tankers a day to dump their ballast water taken from Los Angeles, Long Beach and other tropical ports the clams disappeared and were replaced with sea weed and algae that choked everything to death. There are no clams anywhere in Kachemak bay except way up the bay by Bear cove and the state is allowing clam diggers to wipe them out so there will be no renewable resource left and no chance to reseed them after the oil tankers depart. Why is government destroying food resources? Is it for societal control?

In addition to the crab fishery we also lost the clam resource due to state greed and lust for big money to billions in oil leases. They brought millions of invasive species to Alaska.

Calerpa Taxifolia

Caulerpa Taxifolia is a killer sew weed and the GENUS has more than 70 species including those found in pet stores. It can also survive in cold water and live up to ten days out of water if kept damp. The growth rate is astounding and it covers the beaches with a smothering coat of slime. It's a gorgon weed that could possibly take over the entire world and this state allowed it to be brought into what at one time was referred to as the most productive bay in the world; Kachemak Bay.

It can also reproduce sexually and the eggs can travel with the tide causing it to spread faster than any other known algae.

Killer Alga, Caulerpa taxifolia

The Situation: Caulerpa taxifolia is an invasive alga that is causing serious environmental problems in the Mediterranean Sea. This invasive weed was discovered in southern California and New South Wales, Australia in 2000. Caulerpa taxifolia was officially eradicated from southern California in 2006.

Caulerpa taxifolia is native in tropical waters with populations naturally occurring in the Caribbean, Gulf of Guinea, Red Sea, East African coast, Maldives, Seychelles, northern Indian Ocean, southern China Sea, Japan, Hawai'i, Fiji, New Caledonia and tropical/sub-tropical Australia. A cold water strain of this attractive tropical alga, possibly developed from plants that initially originated from Australia, was selected for by aquarium managers at the Wilhelma Zoo in Stuttgart, Germany in 1980. By 1984, this coldwater strain of Caulerpa had been released into the Mediterranean Sea by the Oceanographic Museum of Monaco where it established.

A meadow of Caulerpa taxifolia in the Mediterranean sea. Dense fields of this invasive alga smother other species and biodiversity declines.Currently, Caulerpa has colonized thousands of hectares of sea bottom in the Mediterranean and it is found from France to Croatia and its range in the Mediterranean will likely to continue to expand. The invasive strain of Caulerpa can tolerate low sea water temperatures and can survive out of water, in moist conditions, for up to 10 days. This alga can colonize most kinds of substrates including rock, sand, mud, and seagrass beds from depths ranging from less than 1 m to ~12 m.

Caluerpa is capable of rapid growth and reproduction of the invasive strain is asexual and dispersal occurs through fragmentation. Fragments as small as 1 cm give raise to viable plants. Long distance spread occurs via ballast water discharge from transoceanic boats and illegal dumping of aquaria plants. More localized dispersal occurs through the unintentional movement of plant material on boats, anchors, or fishing gear, or via algal fragments being dispersed by sea currents.

The Problem: The invasive strain of Caulerpa in the Mediterranean Sea smothers other algal species, seagrasses and sessile invertebrate communities. It does this by either out-competing species for food and light or due to the toxic effects of caulerpenyne compounds that are contained in its foliage. Large meadows of Caulerpa have vastly reduced native species diversity and fish habitat. Native fish which are able to eat Caulerpa, such as Mediterranean bream, accumulate caulerpenyne toxins in their flesh which makes these fish unsuitable for human consumption.

The appearance of Caluerpa in southern California in 2000 was most probably caused by an aquarium owner improperly dumping the contents of a marine fish tank into a storm water system that fed into Agua Hedionda Lagoon in Carlsbad where this weed was first discovered. California has since passed a law forbidding the possession, sale or transport of Caulerpa taxifolia within the state. There is also a federal law under the Noxious Weed Act forbidding interstate sale and transport of the aquarium strain Caulerpa. Caulerpa Distribution in CA Map

When first detected the populations of Caulerpa in southern California were small enough for eradication to be feasible. To eradicate underwater populations of Caulpera, patches were covered with tarpaulins which were held down with sandbags which sealed the edges. Chlorine was poured under the sealed tarpaulins which trapped the chlorine. Chlorine in this instance acted as a pesticide and killed living organisms trapped under the tarpaulins, including Caulerpa. The unintentional killing of fish, invertebrates, and plants while not desirable was deemed necessary and preferable to letting Caulpera spread unchecked.

> Economic Impact: Small infestations found in Agua Hedionda Lagoon in Carlsbad near San Diego and Huntington Beach near Los Angeles, took six years to eradicate at a cost of more than $7 million (US). So far no other infestations of the cold water strain of Caulerpa have been located in the USA. In the Mediterranean commercially important fisheries have

been adversely affected because fewer fish live in areas with heavy Caulerpa infestations.

---Center for Invasive Species Research,
University of California Riverside Text and provided
by Mark Hoddle

How fast do algae reproduce?

"Among the oldest forms of life on Earth, algae are single-celled organisms that grow in water and have evolved over billions of years to become the most efficient producers of plant oils.

Like other plants and organisms, algae use photosynthesis to turn light, carbon dioxide and a few nutrients into the oils, carbohydrates and proteins that make up their cell structure.

Are all algae the same?

No. While there are thousands of different species, algae can be broadly categorized into two main types. One type, microalgae, are microscopic organisms that live in water as single cells or in colonies. Microalgae grow fast, and some can double in size in 24 hours."

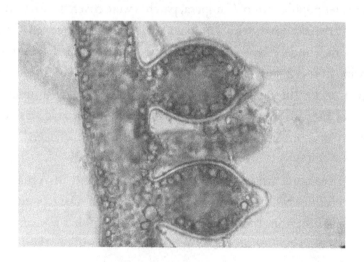

I got into a rather heated argument with a retired lawyer how dumping twenty-million gallons of oil tanker ballast water into Cook

Inlet every day can possibly have any effect on the water toxicity and adverse effect on plankton blooms. His side of the argument was that lower Cook Inlet has such a large volume of water that 20-million gallons a day of oil tanker ballast water would have little or no effect on the environment.

I couldn't argue this fact at the time. What he didn't understand was that biological organisms like algae can reproduce at a very rapid rate and some of them can double in size and volume in only 12 hours.

All of Cook Inlet with an average depth of 40-fthoms (200-feet) and an average width of 30-miles and spawning beds about 60 miles equals 1,800 square miles equals about 68 cubic miles. It moves up and down the inlet about 48 miles so there isn't that much circulation. It's the same old polluted water moving up and down the inlet 48 miles. Given the fact that algae, nematode and bacteria reproduce at a fast rate it would take but a couple years to alter the entire food chain and plankton blooms making it impossible for king crab, tanner crab, Dungeness crab and shrimp to survive.

In addition to the above mention pollution thousands of tons of road salt dumped on the highways each year. You got hundreds of thousands of gallons antifreeze used to defrost jet planes and car antifreeze dumped near Cook Inlet at the Anchorage International Airport. All that foreign material winds up in Cook Inlet. Then the super-educated high-paid NOAA employees wonder why the beluga whale numbers in Cook Inlet are dwindling...

Encyclopedia Britannica Online:

Sexual reproduction is characterized by the process of meiosis, in which progeny cells receive half of their genetic information from each parent cell. Sexual reproduction is usually regulated by environmental events. In many species, when temperature, salinity, inorganic nutrients (e.g., phosphorus, nitrogen, and magnesium), or day length become unfavorable, sexual reproduction is induced. A sexually reproducing organism typically has two phases in its life cycle. In the first stage, each cell has a single set of chromosomes and is called haploid, whereas in the second stage each cell has two sets of chromosomes and is called diploid. When one haploid gamete fuses with another haploid gamete during fertilization, the resulting combination, with two sets of chromosomes, is called a zygote. Either immediately or at some later time, a diploid cell directly or indirectly undergoes a special reductive cell-division process (meiosis). Diploid cells in this stage are called sporophytes because they produce spores. During meiosis the chromosome number of a diploid sporophyte is halved, and the resulting daughter cells are haploid. At some time, immediately or later, haploid cells act directly as gametes. In algae, as in plants, haploid cells in this stage are called gametophytes because they produce gametes

In my book COSMOLOGICAL ICE AGES I mentioned the fact that diatoms can multiply eight times in 24 hours give 24-hours of light and enough food. Diatomaceous Earth is the white powder that you filter your drinking water with through their dead bodies. They have evolved different shapes like snowflakes to take advantage of different wave lengths of light at the various depths of water. Given their ability to reproduce they can fill up an entire ocean with Diatomaceous Earth in a couple years. The only limiting factor is food and light.

Also, when you introduce a foreign specie into the environment there are few or no predators to keep it in check so it can take over very fast and choke other species to death. Hundreds of millions of foreign species of bacteria, algae and nematodes were introduce into Cook. We saw a dramatically decline in the crab and shrimp in only ten years.

Why are the beaches dead in Seldovia bay when they used to be alive with worms, centipedes and big white hard shell clams that the people depended on for food? When you have a government that claims ownership of all natural resources then Government is responsible for the destruction of a billion-dollar a year fishery that was harvested by the private sector. When will they admit they were responsible?

HERE IS WHAT HAPPENS DURING AN OIL SPILL

Copied from AMERICA'S RIVERS THREATS & SOLUTIONS --
PIPELINE COMPANY GIVES UP ON CLEANING ITS OIL SPILL

Update: Feb 6, 2015 Three weeks after the Poplar
Pipeline spewed 40,000 gallons of oil into the
Yellowstone River in eastern Montana, cleanup efforts
have been called off due to dangerous ice conditions.
The spill, which occurred on January 17, contaminated
the city of Glendive's drinking water supply and sickened
local residents. It was the... Read more --Scott Bosse |
January 23, 2015

Scott Bosse UPDATE: FEB 6, 2015

Three weeks after the Poplar Pipeline spewed 40,000 gallons of
oil into the Yellowstone River in eastern Montana, cleanup efforts
have been called off due to dangerous ice conditions. The spill, which
occurred on January 17, contaminated the city of Glendive's drinking
water supply and sickened local residents. It was the second major
oil pipeline spill in the Yellowstone River in four years. In July 2011,
Exxon's Silvertip Pipeline dumped 63,000 gallons of oil into the river
near Laurel, Montana.

During the abbreviated cleanup, a total of 1,200 gallons of oil was
allegedly recovered from the river. At the peak of the cleanup effort, a
spokesman for the company that operates the Poplar Pipeline said that
oil was being recovered at the rate of one teaspoon every ten minutes.
At that pace, it would have taken 1,753 years to remove all the oil from
the river.

The Poplar Pipeline, like hundreds of pipelines that cross underneath
the nation's rivers, was constructed in the 1950s and buried just eight
feet under the bed of the Yellowstone River when it was last inspected in
2012. Federal regulations require that pipelines be buried only four feet

underneath rivers despite evidence that large rivers like the Yellowstone can scour 40 feet deep during floods and ice jams.

JANUARY 24, 2015

Nearly a week has passed since an oil pipeline ruptured underneath the bed of the Yellowstone River in eastern Montana, contaminating drinking water supplies for the 6,000 residents of Glendive, sickening several people, and taking an unknown toll on fish and wildlife. Since 1986, pipeline oil spills have caused more than 55 deaths, 2,500 injuries, and more than $7.7 billion in damages.

According to a Houston Chronicle investigation, more than half of the major natural gas transmission lines in Texas were laid more than 40 years ago and now are vulnerable to failure. Nationwide, the issue of pipeline safety took on more urgency in September, when a natural gas transmission line exploded in San Bruno, Calif., killing eight people and destroying three dozen homes. The National Transportation Safety Board said it has not ruled out pipeline age, or associated problems with welds and corrosion, as potential causes. The Pacific Gas & Electric Co. pipeline in San Bruno was installed in 1956.

In Texas alone, more than 25,000 of nearly 46,000 miles of transmission pipe are older than 1970, some dating to the Great Depression, according to federal records. Federal regulators warned companies more than 20 years ago to reconsider the use of all pipelines built with lower-quality welding techniques that were widely employed in pipe factories prior to 1970, documents show. Also a potential problem is some aged protective coating on pipes that actually can make them more vulnerable to corrosion, according to a number of pipeline experts.

CHAPTER EIGHT

The Salmon Will Be Gone Next

The state allowed at least four hundred small outboard powered boats to dip net salmon between the first bend in the river to the bypass bridge. Each fifty-cubic-inch outboard running at an average speed of 2000 RPM discharges 100,000 cubic inches of carbon monoxide through the propeller hub into the river water every minute. Divide 100,000 cubic inches by the number of inches in a cubic foot= 1728 cubic feet per minute = 57.8 cubic feet per minute.

Multiply this times the number of minutes in an hour = 3472.22 cubic feet per hour discharged into the river. Multiply this by twelve hours = 41,666 cubic feet per day. Multiply this by five hundred boats running up and down the river you get 20,833,333 cubic feet of carbon dioxide a day discharged into the river water. Multiply the twenty-million, eight-hundred thirty-three-thousand-three-hundred-three times the number of days in a month = 31 = over 644 million cubic feet a month poison gas discharged into the water in one month.

Five hundred outboard motors with an average of fifty horse power = 25,000 horse power.

Then add the occasional jet boat powered by large V-8 gas engines developing 400 HP with wet exhausts running up the river at high speed leaving huge wakes behind their boats erodes the muddy river banks away depositing thousands of tons of sediment into the water. Normally the river banks are smooth but after the dip net season starts the river bank has steps cut into it by the wakes from all the boats. How many thousand tons of fine sediment is released into the river water when five-hundred boats with a total of 25,000 horsepower are running up and down the river for one month is anybody's guess.

The salmon have to swim through this poison gauntlet and breathe the water. When the water is filled with fine sediment their gills get coated with mud causing them to pump their gills harder thereby taking in more carbon monoxide and carbon dioxide when they traverse the six miles from two miles off the mouth of the river to the bridge. We don't know how much CO_2 and carbon dioxide is absorbed into the blood stream of the salmon and into the eggs. We don't know the affect this will have on the eggs when they hatch. Will the salmon fry be smaller? Will they be sick with poison? Will a larger percentage of them die before they return to the ocean? Will they be smaller than average? Will they be more susceptible to ocean predation? We don't know because we have no data on any of this.

Commercial boats do not pollute the water as much because they discharge their exhaust gas into the air and generally run up and down river at a slower pace allowing the salmon to get out of the way.

Then there are the prop strikes. How many salmon are killed by propellers slicing into the heads and bodies of the salmon is anybody's guess. We have no data on this. Then there is the fact that half the subsistence salmon are wasted by the consumers as they leave them in their freezers for a year and then clean out the freezers when the next season starts taking them to the dump to make room for the next years catch.

Me.

The fall floods we have been having the last couple years wash a lot of the salmon eggs out of the nests. The floods also wash all the dead salmon carcasses out of the lakes and streams so that the cocoapod bloom in the spring has little fertilizer to grow on. When the few remaining fry have little or nothing to eat they starve and or leave the river about half the size that they should be. Salmon fry don't survive well in the open ocean when they are undersized and weak from mal-nutrition. When in this condition they don't have enough strength to escape from predators.

Feeder fish like the king salmon and silvers have to eat polluted needle fish and herring with big cancer sores on their sides. What the herring and needle fish have to eat is the wrong food composed of foreign organisms brought in by oil tankers from other parts of the world. They also migrate further out into the Pacific Ocean further than any other species of salmon. They also stay in the remote Pacific area up to eight years. The radioactive liquid and flotsam from three Japanese Fukishima atomic reactors circulates in a gyre where king salmon spend up to eight years eating the zoo plankton and herring.

From left to right: Henry Kroll Senior, Brother, Herb Kroll who passed away in 1974. I am on the far right. We fish across Cook Inlet eighty miles south southwest from the Kenai River. Delbert Phillips is sitting on the rail waiting to unload his small catch. He looks rather dejected.

Me and Herb 1968.

Public officials coming to Alaska from New York, Peoria, Illinois and other places to find jobs are unfamiliar with the Culture and the knowledge necessary to make a living in Bush Alaska. They would never understand my father who worked two 24-hour days picking salmon then sleep 12-hours and get up and fish another 48 hours. I worked right alongside of him and remember that on the second day my legs hurt so bad that I could barely stand. I remember picking over 600 fish an hour racing the tide to keep the skiff from going dry. I would work so hard that foam come out of my mouth like an overworked draft horse. We did it to feed our families through the winter. We get no respect from this COURT because it doesn't understand and never will.

In the 1950's and 60's my father and I worked many 24-hour days proving up on the original homestead United States Survey 4685 in Tuxedni Bay. I worked ten years helping his father to prove up on the homestead clearing land, pulling stumps, planting timothy hay, clover and planting trees.

My brother Herbert Kroll was born 12/19/1946 fished salmon all his life. He purchased a new 32-drift boat PENGA from Commercial Marine in Seattle POWERED BY A NEW 130 HP PERKENS DIESEL, ran it north to Alaska to discover the newly formed Commercial Fishery Entry Commission made up of out of state bureaucrats wouldn't give him a salmon permit. He tried to make a living fishing halibut with his new gillnetter when Halibut was selling for only 12 cents a pound and had to quit. He could not work at a regular job sue to a nervous disorder and shot himself in the head with a 357 caliber pistol 9/14/1974. This same Commercial Fishery Entry Commission gave over 100 salmon drift permits to foreign immigrants coming to Alaska.

Below is a document stating that the CFEC issued an interim use drift permit to Herbert Kroll dated 1/27/1974. I believe they printed this document to cover their ass because Herb had sold his boat the year before and killed himself 9/14/1974. How evil is that?

The next document is a letter from the CFEC denying that they ever issued a salmon fishing drift permit to Herbert Kroll. How evil is that?

STATE OF ALASKA
COMMERCIAL FISHERIES ENTRY COMMISSION
1974 INTERIM-USE PERMIT NO. H2-03-21478
IN ACCORDANCE WITH THE REGULATION OF ENTRY INTO
ALASKA COMMERCIAL FISHERIES

Herbert H. Kroll

Halibut Cove c/o Homer,

Alaska 99603

SOCIAL   DATE OF
SECURITY NO. 574-18-8163   BIRTH 12/19/1946

HAS BEEN ISSUED AN INTERIM-USE PERMIT TO OPERATE A
UNIT OF *Drift Gill Net GEAR IN ADMINISTRATIVE
AREA "H" Cook Inlet.

COMMERCIAL FISHERIES ENTRY COMMISSION

BY   DATE 1/27/74

SIGNATURE OF
PERMIT HOLDER

THIS PERMIT IS VALID THROUGH DECEMBER 31, 1974. APPLICATION
FOR 1975 RENEWAL OF INTERIM-USE PERMIT OR FOR A PERMANENT
PERMIT, WHICHEVER IS APPLICABLE, MUST BE MADE PRIOR TO
JANUARY 1, 1975.

THE PERMIT HOLDER MUST HAVE THE PERMIT IN HIS POSSESSION
AT ALL TIMES WHEN ENGAGED IN THE OPERATION OF THE GEAR
FOR WHICH IT WAS ISSUED.

01-801

FORM A   APPLICATION FOR ENTRY PERMIT
ALASKA COMMERCIAL FISHERIES ENTRY COMMISSION
IMPORTANT: READ INSTRUCTIONS BEFORE COMPLETING THIS FORM

They jerked him around five years before he killed himself. He also fished our set-net sites and had a set-net permit # H-165. What ever happened to that permit?

What will happen to the salmon?

The phytoplankton grows in this area and the zoo plankton eat the phytoplankton thereby concentrating any radioactive poisons ten to one then the king salmon eat the zoo plankton concentrating the radioactive poisons ten more times. We don't know what affect this will have on future generations of king salmon. We don't know what effect this will have on the people who eat the king salmon. Will their prostates glow in the dark? Will you be able to find their graves with a Geiger counter after they die?

Then you have the 20-million gallons per day sewage from Anchorage, Palmer and Wasilla and toxic chemicals. The criminals running this state caused us to lose a billion-dollar a year crab and shrimp fishery. The salmon will be next. It is a crime what they are doing with four hundred outboards discharging exhaust gas into the water of the Kenai River.

The solution to saving the salmon is to have people use row boats or electric outboards thereby eliminating all the carbon monoxide pollution and reducing the amount of sediment being washed out of the river banks. This will allow the salmon to swim through relatively clean water except for the salmon guts, urine and sewage being dumped into the river by the occupants of the dip net boats.

Author's wife, Mary, Woogey, Gabbie and Sasha

The author and his 220 HP Maule with Gar Aero tires.

CHAPTER NINE

State Government Formed
To Take Resources

I was born in Seldovia, Alaska in 1944. I was here when the state government was formed in 1959. I distinctly remember talk about hiring foreign workers for ten dollars and hour to harvest salmon thereby cheating residents who had been fishing for a living many decades out of their only livelihood. Socialist governments can never get it through their heads that people working for low wages are not as productive as people who think they are working for themselves. Communism responsible for the deaths of 200-million people has been proven not to work time after time. The very definition of insanity is "doing the same thing over and over again expecting different results."

The State of Alaska is an anti-American, abusive, criminal enterprise that systematically violated our constitutional rights. America was built on celebrating Freedom from Government, not dependency on it. The State of Alaska has violated its constitution multiple times by allowing big corporations to destroy the fisheries. Oil transport companies were allowed to dump trillions of gallons of their bacteria and algae contaminated tanker ballast water taken from the foreign ports of Korea, Japan, Hawaii, Los Angeles, San Francisco and Anacortes, Washington.

Worse still, the STATE OF ALASKA contracted courts are the only government agency that can launch an investigation, make an accusation, render a verdict, and impose a punishment—without ANY oversight or checks and balances. The STATE OF ALASKA COURTS ACT as cops, prosecutors, judge, jury and executioner all rolled up into one!

I will try to make this book as concise as possible, yet, fill in some of the gaps that the news media has left out. It's about how billions of dollars were stolen from the private sector and how the livelihood of citizens has been destroyed by shortsighted greed and corruption. How the state destroyed a billion dollar a year renewable fishery resources to keep billions of dollars from large corporations going into various foreign bank accounts.

So where did the government spend the trillion dollars of resources they stole from the people? There are entire books on how bureaucracies operate. First you appoint someone who is not an elected representative of the people to some important desk job; like, "Commissioner of this or that department of etc., etc." They have to have a large salary commensurate with their level of incompetence and an operating budget. Their office should be further away from the seat of government the better because there is less oversight. As the years go by the important department heads have to have more secretaries and more office space to process the ever increasing piles of paperwork. Soon they occupy the entire floor of a large office building.

Picture this scenario fifty years into the future to the year 2017. Now we have 50 of more of these non-elected department heads overseeing the dispersal of resources, loans, and bogus environmental offices each with their own army of secretaries occupying fifty or more office buildings in several major cities. How is anyone going to oversee and control the graft and corruption that such a system breeds?

Three decades ago there was an Anchorage Times article where a reporter had visited Juneau where they have a machine that cuts the state paychecks. He picked up a handful of check stubs off the floor and noticed that they had Swiss bank account numbers on them. Some of the checks were made out to Mickey Mouse, Donald Duck, Pluto and Goofy for amounts varying from $18,000 up to $75,000.00. He printed the article but their excuse was the people working on the check cutting floor were merely testing the equipment. If that were so then, why were there Swiss bank account numbers on the check stubs?

Professional negotiators representing big corporations actually run this state. Do you actually think that elected officials from the boondocks have the business experience and acumen to negotiate business deals that would be favorable for the state? We're at a point now where all the corporations have to do is threaten to pull their business out of Alaska and the Legislature will give them a hundred-million dollars. The state recently gave Trans Canada 500-million dollars. Our elected officials have let the wolves loose in the hen house. "The Cardinal rule of a bureaucrat is they can never admit a wrong."

We fishermen lost a billion dollars-worth of boats and gear. We couldn't provide for our families and some of our kids were put into boarding schools. Families were forced to file for welfare. Many skippers were divorced and became alcoholics. Many processing plants had to close down in the villages and towns around Kodiak Island and Seldovia. Whole families of Pilipino cannery workers and native Alaskans had to relocate to Anchorage and other cities to find work. The stress and hardship inflected on residents was horrendous.

The state allowed the depletion of its renewable resources to get rid of fishermen so there was no opposition to selling oil leases in lower Cook Inlet and Kodiak waters. After years of seismic work and oil companies had little or no interested in drilling in those areas so the whole corrupt experiment was and exercise in futility.

During the lawsuit I filed 22 affidavits documenting these facts and my personal losses when a state agency stole my business plan to make surimi and kamaboko (fake crab legs made from Pollock) and wasted another five-million dollars to buy a fish plant to make it in.

This is how you get rich in Alaska!

Alaska Renewable Resources Corporation (ARRC) a state loan corporation gave a few million to one of their relatives working at ARRC to buy the Gibson Cove fish plant south of Kodiak city. A lot of nepotism goes on within state agencies when big money is involved. They like to share the wealth at private sector expense. They don't care who they put out of business.

The 40-million dollar fish plant the state of Alaska constructed near the International Airport in Anchorage is another example of the state government trying to compete with the private sector. They can't make a profit because in every case they are overcapitalized. The equipment they purchase with unlimited funds uses too much electricity or requires too much expensive maintenance thereby cutting into profits. After the plant sat idle for eight years they gave the huge buildings away to the Baptist Church. There are too many of these examples to cover in this book such as the Matanuska Maid dairy, the high speed ferry from Nikiski to Anchorage, the state-owned barley storage buildings in Seward etc., Etc.

Anyway, I kept sending my affidavits into the court and nobody rebutted them so I recorded a commercial lien of 65-million dollars documenting my losses. I had a copy of a vessel survey for my process ship Orion listing its replacement values of $4,500,000.00. In commercial liens you are allowed to claim three times your losses so that brought the total up to over 65-million dollars. Needless to say none of the participants and their crooked lawyers liked my commercial lien. The judge tried to interfere with my liens saying they were Common Law liens. That is a matter of opinion not fact.

Several times I made motions by special appearance for reconsideration with demand that the Court support the ruling with findings of fact and conclusions of law, and in the absence of same that the rulings be stricken as unsupported opinion, frivolous, void, and not binding in this Court. I asked that the Court submit a Law or statute used to determine that Henry Kroll had no claim to the spit/tideland/

island in Tuxedni Bay west and south of US Survey 4685. It refused to submit any law or statute. This Court was unable to support the ruling with law, so its COURT ORDERS are of necessity frivolous, without merit, and not binding in ANY COURT.

Years ago I made a MOTION for this Court to submit a copy of its OATH, CONTRACT and BOND. This court refused to respond to my motion. By that default there is no subject matter jurisdiction and should have dismissed this case at that time. If this Court had an Oath it would be required to be impartial. With due respect, upon what facts, law and evidence do you base your statement or ruling?

An administrative ruling by a CONTRACT COURT working FOR the state of Alaska is a rebellion against BOTH STATE AND FEDERAL CONSTITUTIONS and is frivolous, without merit, and not binding. By refusing to support and abide by the Constitutions this COURT is not real but is an INQUISITION where the innocent are penalized for no reason. Any Officer of the Court who exceeds his authority of his office or steps outside his OATH must vacate his office and lose his immunity and pension.

I made several MOTIONS for dismissal of this case for lack of subject matter jurisdiction and it failed to respond to my motions. By that default, the parties are in agreement, and no controversy exists for adjudication, hence there is no subject matter jurisdiction and no case. I requested, "Please dismiss immediately as this motion was unopposed.

I believe that **impeding due process of rights** by making preemptive administrative judgment rulings against defendants before they can respond to Plaintiff's MOTIONS for the purpose of stopping them from defending themselves is not only a violation of COURT RULES it is a crime punishable by a year in prison. Preemptive judgments before Defendants can respond with opposing MOTIONS is a violation of COURT RULES and CONTEMPT OF COURT. It is practicing 'COLOR OF LAW' Title 18 U.S. C., SECTION 242 **shall be fined under this title or imprisoned not more than one year, or both:**

From the DOJ website itself.

> "TITLE 18, U.S.C., SECTION 242
> Whoever, under color of any law, statute, ordinance, regulation, or custom, willfully subjects any person in any State, Territory, Commonwealth, Possession, or District to the deprivation of any rights, privileges, or immunities secured or protected by the Constitution or laws of the United States,... shall be fined under this title or imprisoned not more than one year, or both; and if bodily injury results from the acts committed in violation of this section or if such acts include the use, attempted use, or threatened use of a dangerous weapon, explosives, or fire, shall be fined under this title or imprisoned not more than ten years, or both; and if death results from the acts committed in violation of this section or if such acts include kidnaping or an attempt to kidnap, aggravated sexual abuse, or an attempt to commit aggravated sexual abuse, or an attempt to kill, shall be fined under this title, or imprisoned for any term of years or for life, or both, or may be sentenced to death." http://www.justice.gov/crt/about/crm/242fin.ph

Color (law) From Wikipedia, the free encyclopedia (Redirected from Color of law)

In United States law, the term color of law denotes the "mere semblance of legal right", the "pretense or appearance of" right; hence, an action done under color of law colors (adjusts) the law to the circumstance, yet said apparently legal action contravenes the law.[1] Under color of authority is a legal phrase used in the US[2] indicating that a person is claiming or implying the acts he or she is committing are related to and legitimized by his or her role as an agent of governmental power, especially if the acts are unlawful.

The unambiguous Statute of Alaska codified in AS: 22.05.140, to wit:

> "(b) A salary disbursement may not be issued to a justice or judge until the justice or judge has filed with the state officer designated to issue the disbursements an affidavit that no matter referred to the justice for opinion of decision had been uncompleted or undecided by the justice or judge for a period of more than six months."

The SUPRIOR COURT "FOR" THE STATE OF ALASKA judge William Morse working "FOR" THE STATE OF ALASKA sat on my case more than twelve years.

What is a State?

State of Alaska is an act of congress signed by President Eisenhower. Can anyone prove that a piece of paper is the owner of land? Can you prove that henry-f-kroll the live human is living in or on that piece of paper?

Oath of allegiance = protection

If a state really wants to protect life, liberty or property then why is it the first to take these things away? [Obviously the government has no obligation to protect you]

What is a case? Shaney v county of Winnebago "If there is no duty to protect anybody then there is no allegiance and no Citizens."

Only recently have I been made aware of the duality nature of court proceedings promulgated by the government to gain authority over living human beings. Fact: government is a corporation and corporations have no authority over and cannot sue living human beings. It must first fraudulently without their knowledge turn living human beings into corporations by spelling their names in capital letters. It's a sad state of affairs when you can't trust your own government.

WHAT IS COMMON LAW?

I.e. unwritten basically means un-legislated, since it wasn't created by legislature but by people's juries and decisions of judges. You gotta realize that in societies with REAL MONEY in circulation, the State doesn't bring charges, the INJURED party does. He files the charge with a sheriff, who brings the accused to court for trial. Then the JURY decides the guilt and the judge assigns the punishment with accordance with past decisions about the same charge. NO LEGISLATURE or STATE LAW necessary, since the jury of your peers decides the guilt.

So that's COMMON LAW, which is unlike STATUTORY LAW, which was written by a legislature (or a king). BTW, that's why legislatures in the past were TEMPORARY. They only met a few times a year, since they were only administering the public property. Courts handled all the criminal matters, based on the 35 common law crimes.

BTW, you can still see a shade of that today in some places. For example, there's one UNINCORPORATED town here in So. California, and their mayor and city politicians only meet a few times a year. So they have no police, since they don't need it to generate revenue to pay them salary, like all the incorporated cities with full time city councils need. And with no police in the town, it's the sheriff to whom you go with criminal complaints. And of course in that town, there are NO CITY ordinances and codes. Only county and state laws apply there.

And so common law was CODIFIED in Criminal code. In USA the Public Law was/is our version of common law. And Public law is ONLY all PRE-1933 laws and court decisions. You know, like all the US Supreme Court decisions declaring income tax unconstitutional, unless apportioned. All POST-1933 laws are NOT Public/common law. They are Public POLICY.

Good example are gun and drug laws. Under common law, what you buy (with REAL money) belongs to you UNCONDITIONALLY. Under statutory law, what you buy (with debt notes), is subject to State regulation (Statutory law). That's why prior to 1913, there were NO DRUG and GUN laws, since people still had gold money.

What's the difference? Public Law is of the de jure REPUBLIC, and is divided into AT LAW and EQUITY jurisdiction. Public Policy on the other hand, is of the corporate DEMOCRACY, and is administered under STATUTORY jurisdiction. You know, Article III courts vs Article I courts.

And what's the difference btw. Republic and Democracy? Republic uses REAL gold money, while Democracy uses DEBT NOTES (FRNs) as money. And real money give you real allodial ownership, while debt notes just give you a CONDITIONAL ownership, which is subject to State regulation. In a Republic, when it comes to ownership, the State ONLY regulates commodities and commerce. In Democracy the State regulates EVERYTHING.

Common Law was referred to as "judge made law" because the jury is the judge and they have the right to judge both the law and the facts which is how they kept the legislatures in line - they would not convict on law they did not approve of - they did not convict their fellow man on a law they believed unfair and that they themselves would not want to be charged with - this was brought forward when they had to repeal the 18th amendment on alcohol - the people would not convict - that is why the "savings to suitors" clause preserved remedies to convene a common law court - Senate Report 94-1148 is the legislative history of Bretton Woods and specifically says the "unauthorized transition" to floating parity on the US dollar is unconstitutional

I wish to add that more accurately the Common Law was derived from the Common Lore. And just that there is a common law of the legal society (Kolender Case Law) otherwise known as English Common Law, and there is American Common Law (unwritten lore, common amongst the people): see John Locke; Two Treatises of Government.

The common law writ of mandamus was codified in California under c.c.p. 1085. When there is no remedy, this is the remedy! Thus: the beauty of the common law always giving a remedy. Demurrer is also a common law remedy codified in California at penal codes 1002-1012.

CHAPTER TEN

Communism Defined
from my book SURVIVING THE NEW WORLD ORDER

Communism is currently responsible for the death of over 200-million people. The writers of the Communist Manifesto copied the idea from the ancient writings of Plato's Republic who dreamed up a utopian society where everybody was compensated equally regardless of how hard they worked or how important and valuable their contributions to society were as a whole. For avowed Communists free enterprise and profit are DIRTY words, since they want everybody to be EQUAL. And by that they DON'T mean equal rights. NOOO, they mean equal INCOME!

In their puny brains they CAN'T STAND it when one man has more money or more property than another. This is a MAJOR case of ENVY. Like the BORG in the Star Trek they want to ASSIMILATE you into their HIVE society, or eliminate you. **Why do you think that Obama, Nancy Pelosi, Harry Reid and other liberals are so hell-bent on banning guns??? If you can't defend your family Communism is what you will get!**

Here's an example of how communism operates in the real world. Communists in Soviet Union first BANNED GUN OWNERSHIP. There were millions of people there who lived by GROWING THEIR FOOD on a few acres of land they owned. But that made them too independent for the commies to tolerate. They wanted them to give up their land and join big, gov't-controlled collectivist farms.

But since millions weren't interested in doing that, **the commies sent the military to confiscated their SEEDS. The people then couldn't grow any food, and millions died of hunger. They were basically MURDERED by the communist government, so their land could be confiscated by the collectivist farms. Over eighty million people died in the Soviet Union as a result. China murdered close to 100-million...**

The ultimate goal of all communists; OUTLAWING private property and even OUTLAWING MONEY. And what happens when the commie gov't outlaws money, growing food and even barter? **You'll have to come to the gov't for food**. And they'll tell you, sure but you gotta work, and here's the job we have for you and **you don't get paid so you become a slave!**

So you're basically a SLAVE of the government. Here's another example of communism, although they called it socialism, in Cambodia in **1976**: *"The Khmer Rouge transformed Cambodia into a rural, classless society in which there were no rich people and no poor people. (Sound familiar?)*

They abolished money, free markets, normal schooling, private property and religious practices. All Public schools, churches, universities, shops and government buildings were closed or turned into prisons, stables, "reeducation" camps and granaries. There was also to be no public or private transportation! The citizens would no longer need it! All people would now live and work in the countryside, together, as equals, for the new Cambodian state!

Pol Pot summed up the policy himself saying: "We are building socialism." The Khmer Rouge banned family relationships. Children were to be raised, as good Socialists, by the state, not by their parents. Some were placed in separate forced labor camps, some in interrogation centers out of contact with their parents: Family influence was not good for the collective wellbeing. The family unit was dead.

All food was now to be grown on communal farms and, with the Khmer Rouge's distain of all (capitalist) modern technology, people *__were forced to farm by hand.__* This made it impossible for workers to reach the rice quotas imposed by the Socialists!

The people could only eat the tiny portions of "watery rice" that were allotted to them.

Everyone got them same amount. (Socialism) Most of the rice was being sent to Khmer Rouge soldiers and political leaders. __*If anyone was caught supplementing their diet, with leafs, bugs or anything, they would be beaten, tortured, sent to prison or killed on the spot.*__ __Like I said, under communism you OWN NOTHING, and MUST turn everything to the STATE OF ALASKA/TRIBE. Eating ANYTHING without the tribe's permission is a CRIME.__

__The daily ration was so low it would cause hundreds of thousands of people to starve to death.__ Khmer Rouge cadres would also look for any excuse to kill "new people" (city people) as they arrived.

Minority groups and suspected capitalists were the intended targets but, as with all Communist / Socialists societies, __this also included any "new" civilians that just happened to arrive.__

__Anyone who was suspected of being educated including doctors, teachers, engineers, lawyers, scientists and professional people,__ *along with their extended families,* __*were killed because they were considered enemies of the state.*__

> __*If you spoke French, you would die.*__
> __*If you were educated, you would die.*__
> __*If you wore glasses, you would die.*__
> __*If you practiced religion, you would die.*__

The tortures were inhumane and death was the normal result." __This is pretty much what hardcore liberals like Barack Obama and Hillary Clinton wanted to implement should they remain in power. You know, people who HATE capitalism and freedom, and want to force their communist HELL on everyone, in the name of EQUALITY, protecting animals and protecting the planet; and ATTACK THE FIRST AND SECOND AMENDMENTS of the Constitution.__

So I hope you realize that **what commies want is to REVERT back to a TRIBAL society, where PRIVATE ownership is ILLEGAL, and EVERYTHING is owned by the STATE.** Or on a larger scale, it's owned by the GOVERNMENT. So whatever you find, earn, or acquire, you MUST turn over to the tribe/gov't. It DOESN'T belong to you, and keeping it is a CRIME. If a lower class, surf in the Middle Ages invented something, it belonged to the Lord, Baron, Earl, Duke or King.

The Alaskan government isn't pure Communism in that we have elected official with term limits but the people who gravitate to these positions of power are usually those who want to control others so they —enact many thousands of laws controlling every aspect of your life! Most of them are not from Alaska. They came here to seek their fortune and they brought with them their culture and ideas from other socialist states. It is because of this they make it their goal to make Alaska exactly like the Hell they came out of.

You can't get married without the state's permission with a marriage license. You can't harvest gold, fish, and tin etc., without applying to some non-elected bureaucrats for a license and paying exorbitant fees, etc.

What will you do when the only means of buying food and gasoline is a plastic card? What will you do when all the Wal-Mart's and Costco's stocked with Chinese goods are closed and we are at war? China? COSCO is: 'Chinese Overseas Shipping Company.' Bit Coins plus silver and gold coins may be your only salvation.

The service life of the Trans-Alaska pipeline was estimated to be twenty-five years. At the present time the pipeline is now 40 years old. When it shuts down due to lack of oil or starts springing thousands of leaks they will have to shut it down and there is no way to clean up the mess.

The Permanent Fund should be put into an irrevocable trust for the people of Alaska. Then we will have to write a new constitution that allows people to own land and resources so that they can support themselves like in other states. Taxing the people for their labor when they are living in poverty won't work. We can't allow the current State government to continue to steal any more of our resources. We have to give the resources back to the people and get away from Communist rule. It hasn't worked in the past and it won't work in the future. It has been proven not to work time after time! There is no use beating a dead horse.

The Author and his J-3 Cub.

CHAPTER ELEVEN

You Can't Handle The Truth!

By henry kroll, living man

One past Borough Mayor goes on to quote a 2003 report for the Alaska Permanent fund Corporation: *"Moreover, the state's revenue structure is such that each additional basic sector job added to the economy ... costs more to state finances than what is generates ... The state must also eradicate the growth-inhibiting incentives of the "Alaska Disconnect," where new non-oil producing employment is a net drag on state finances."*

I believe Mr. Mayor wants us to vote for a state income tax and he doesn't want people to have jobs!

I have seen the "Alaska Disconnect" on public television. When mail is delivered to the Legislator during recess I saw my Legislator throw my letter in the trash. You would think that they would at least open it or wait until the camera was off before they throw your letters in the trash...

The real "Alaska disconnect" is when the state destroys a billion dollar a year crab and shrimp resource by allowing big corporations to dump polluted ballast water taken from foreign ports plus eight oil-well blowouts and then blame the fishermen for overfishing while at the same time paying fish and game biologists to manage the fishery and give them multi-million-dollar research vessels.

After the resources were destroyed and the fishermen lose their boats, filed bankruptcy and divorced their families are forced to go on welfare. The state takes custody of their children turning them into Socialist Democrats completely dependent on government forever. All crab processing plants were forced to shut down in the villages and putting hundreds of cannery workers and villagers out of work and forcing them to relocate to Anchorage and other cities.

After there are no original dollars coming into the economy the towns and villages have to depend on state and federal grants to provide services like sewer, water, fire, police and road maintenance for the remaining few who live in the cities and villages. Seldovia; chartered as a first class city once had five operating fish plants and a population close to three thousand people with five thousand during summer months. Now it has a population of around 200 people and no fish plant and no income except tourism.

Ten years ago it took me over a month to get a copy of the list of non-profits from the Kenai Peninsula Borough. I wanted make a mailing lists of all the churches and other non-profits in the area. The Borough kept making up excuses not to give me the list. When I finally got my hands on the list I was astounded of how many non-profits there are in this area. Counting churches the list totals 645 non-profits. I am sure the list hasn't shrunk any in the last ten years. Every one of the hundred or so municipal corporations in this area including the Kenai Peninsula Borough is a non-profit. The Kenai Police department is a non-profit. The Kenai fire Department is a non-profit. The Soldotna Police is a non-profit. The city of Kenai is a non-profit. The City of Homer is a non-profit. The Alaska State Troopers is a non-profit. Wildwood Prison is a non-profit. The Homer court is a non-profit. Kenai Court is a non-profit. The list goes on and on...

WHY THERE IS A BUDGET CRISIS: YOU CAN'T HANDLE THE TRUTH!

All the hundreds of municipal non-profits in this area are run like an individual business. Each of them has to have an EIN number--an

EMPLOYMENT INDENTIFICATION NUMBER issued by the INTERNAL REVENUE SERVICE. It's kind of like your Social Security Number but for corporations. Each time a municipal corporation writes a payroll check that EIN number is printed on the check making that employee a debt slave responsible to pay the IRS. The state itself even has an EIN number printed on all state checks. The IRS is another private corporation IRS Trust 164 in Puerto Rico. They take all that money and send it to Puerto Rico and half goes to banks in England --- another story.

Keep in mind that municipal corporations are run slightly different from regular corporations. Municipal corporations are bureaucracies. They get their money not from the production but by applying for grants from the state, taxes and fees. In many cases 20% of most grant money is spent on what it was intended while 60% is spent for administration. The corporate heads benefit by it.

The state is another municipal corporation listed on Dunn and Bradstreet. It gets most of its grant money for police and other services from the Federal Government. Attached to most grants are mandates dictating how and how the money is spent.

Besides grant money, municipal corporations collect money from the public they were created to serve; depending on the type of MC, they collect land tax, sales tax, license fees, fishing licenses, dip net permits, parking fees, court fees, fines, charges, speeding tickets, and some create administrative trusts to take money from your birth bond etc. Municipal corporations have to have an office, a bookkeeper, bank accounts, a President, Vice President, Secretaries to type letters, computers, rent, lots of paper etc., etc. In most cases the people who work for non-profit municipal corporations get free health care, paid vacations, day care, maternity leave, paternity leave, sick leave, Christmas bonuses and pension plans and they don't have to work as hard or be productive as people in the private sector.

Depending who is running the municipal corporation, civil service employees seldom if ever are fired. In fact, bureaucracies like incompetent people because then they can hire two or three people to do the same job. The more people they get on their payroll the more powerful they become and the more money they can get from the state and federal governments. If they can take over another public service it gets even better. As the money starts rolling in they hire more and more people to use it up.

According to the book, PETER PRINCIPAL the most incompetent person is kicked upstairs to run the corporation because the more incompetent the boss, the less the people under him have to work... Most civil service workers came here from a bureaucratic, Hells in other states. Their goal is to make it big and retire back home. That is the situation we are in today.... FYI Alaska has more civil service employees per capita than any other state. We are a Socialist Hell State.

Over time people keep voting for more government handouts that require hiring more bureaucrats to dish out free stuff, more licenses, more fees, more taxes, bonds' for infrastructure, sales taxes and fees on everything. There's always a catch where bonds have to be paid back, balloon payments on loans, pension funds etc. After two decades of this nobody has any money left because it's all used up because there are no new original, dollars. Then jobless people wonder the streets wondering what happened. After fifty years of bureaucratic expansion with thousands in retirement those pension plans really add up to where there is no money left for infrastructure, schools, roads, and other services.

Ancient Greece civilization fell when 20% of the population was Civil Service. Rome fell when 25% of the population became Civil Service. Last year Italy's government was in dire straits because they couldn't afford the huge non-producing civil service population. When there aren't enough producers earning original dollars civilizations always collapse. Even banks collapse.

There is no excuse for this to happen in Alaska because we have trillions of dollars in natural resources like diamonds, gold, silver, uranium, tin, iron, coal etc. The Cold War is over. Russia is a poor country. Most of the Cold War was propaganda for societal manipulation to get people behind the manufacture of nuclear arms.

We have the potential for foreign trade with Russia and a tremendous eco-tourism potential across Asia and Europe if they would get the feds to finish the road to Nome. It was surveyed in 1044. All the equipment was lost when a fleet of barges capsized off the coat os Nome in a storm. A road would allow people and small businesses to get to work and we would all have jobs. The present state collective/communist system isn't working and will never work! Only 1% of the land in Alaska is privately owned.

Allow people to get clear title to their land because it has been proven people will work harder to actually own land. --henry kroll, American State Citizen. hankkroll@gmail.com www.GuardDogBooks.com

The Alaska State government has three-million acres of land on the Kenai Peninsula--about two million acres of that virgin land loaded with trace minerals could be used to grow food and lakes to grow fish and crayfish. Thin layers of volcanic ash given off my Redoubt and Augustine volcanoes also contribute some trace minerals.

Given the fact that our Legislators are taking the Permanent Fund to fund an overblown government and borrowing two billion to pay oil companies it's only fair that they allow us to have at least one acre of land per dividend application. You can't have freedom without land ownership. The money stays in the Permanent Fund or pays the Kenai Borough if it is borough land. That way the Permanent fund can grow more.

Getting our kids off the street to tend livestock and learn the value of all life is extremely important. Sitting around most of the day killing zombies and people in computer games does not instill kindness and caring family values. Raising chickens, ducks, geese, pigs, goats, cattle etc. on their own land would keep them out of trouble and connected to the land.

We need your help and contributions to get this message out. Please e-mail this book to everyone you know and send what you can to: Henry Kroll

State income tax a dumb idea

A state income tax is a dumb idea because the State owns all the wealth--all the gold, oil, gas etc., and there are more state employees per catalpa than any other state by a large margin. One in 30 people is currently drawing a state paycheck. You got the railroad, the ferry system, the ferry docks, the bus lines, the state-owned, gold mines, weigh stations, vehicle inspections, fleets of state vehicles, contract courts, court houses, jails, etc., etc., the list is endless....

It is so complicated that I believe our Legislators and Senators don't understand it. For example, many of the checks written by the State Treasury every month go to State contracted non-profits. You got to realize that there are over 700 non-profit corporations here on the Kenai Peninsula alone and about half of them are churches and other organizations not affiliated with the state in any way.

The other non-profits are State non-profits contracted to "work for the state" i.e. Jails, courts, troopers etc., etc. When you go to court is it says SUPERIOR COURT "FOR" THE STATE OF ALASKA it is a non-profit corporation working for the state and they take in lots of extra money by "charging" people as many "charges" as possible and that money goes to the pension funds of the people working there. {They invest some of those funds in Prison Corporation Of America}. If it says SUPERIOR COURT "OF" THE STATE "OF" ALASKA it might be a real court working with real laws not maritime contract law.

I know this is hard for anyone to understand because it goes against everything you were taught in school. Here's the kicker: Each of the State non-profit corporations has to have an Employment Identification Number or EIN number. It's like your Social Security number only it identifies corporations. Now each of those hundreds of non-profit corporations working for the state writes their checks to pay their employees. Each year many of the state non-profits hire additional employees, additional office space, buy new computers, build new office buildings etc., etc. So there is no way to tell how many people are actually working for the State of Alaska. It could be fifty percent of the population for all In know.

Ancient Greece fell when 15% of the population worked as civil service workers. Ancient Rome fell when 20% of the population was civil service. Right now Alaska is around 25%. Nobody knows.

I have an old list of non-profits that I got from the borough in my book store. You would be surprised at what agencies are non-profits.

I wrote in my book **MAKE ALASKA GREAT AGAIN** how the hundreds of sub- corporations working for the state continue to hire more and more people to expand their budget every year. Each of them has their own EIN numbers (employment identification numbers) to pay their employees so that the IRS can keep track of everybody.

All communist governments that own everything eventually fail eventually because they run out of resources and keep on expanding the bureaucracy until they run out of money. It's insane I know, and nobody get it but that's how it works.

They have taken and sold over a trillion dollars of resources since statehood. That's $1,000,000,000,000.00 and built a huge bureaucracy-so large in fact that nobody knows how many state agencies there really are. The State Treasury writes over 17,000 wage checks every month and hundreds of other individual state corporations' pay their employees separate like welfare offices, Lee Shore Agencies, Planned Parenthood, that list is almost endless... and you want a state income tax to pay for all that. A better solution would be to reduce the size of government and let state citizens have access to some of the resources so that they can earn a living.

Do you realize that to collect a State income tax it will require building several more state office buildings in two or more cities to go over 600,000 income tax forms? The end result more than half the money will be used up in administration costs. Some of the paperwork may ever be outsourced to foreign country in a lame attempt to reduce costs. Then you got the time and expense to the private sector paying their accounts to fill out additional forms.

No Communist regime has lasted more than 60 years and next year with be 60-years of Alaska Statehood. The reason they don't last is because eventually the resources and money runs out. Alaska however has millions of acres of land that will keep the bloated bureaucracy going another ten years beyond the 60-year mark. By that time the Permanent fund will be gone and China will own Alaska.

HOW YOUR RESOURCES WERE STOLEN

Constitution for the State of Alaska: Article VIII: Natural Resources

Article VIII is the first article dealing solely and broadly with resources to appear in a state constitution. The delegates wished to curtail what was seen as abuse of Alaska's resources (see Ordinance No. 3) and ensure reasonable development to broaden Alaska's economic base. The chief principle was that resources <u>should be managed as a public trust, providing "for maximum use consistent with the public interest"</u>, further defined as "utilization, development, and conservation... for the maximum benefit of [the] people"; for common access to resources; and for development to be based on sustainable yield. Article VIII also provides for state parks and protected areas, and for the leasing of state lands for resource development.

   <u>What they mean by, 'Public interest' is getting the most money for the state GOVERNMENT, not the public... As people we don't have access to resources but big corporations do! Then they use the money to grow mor government.</u>

One of the aims of the delegates was to produce a short, general document, on the model of the United States Constitution. Rather than specify most aspects in minute detail, as did many state constitutions, the delegates chose instead to leave broad authority to future state legislatures. The resulting document is thus only half the average state constitution length of 26,000 words.

   When you give this much power to Legislatures to sell (rip off) resources, the money DISSAPPEARS. WE VOTED TO MOVE THE CAPITOL OF ALASKA FOUR TIMES!!!

DON'T YOU THINK THE POLITICANS SHOULD ABIDE
BY A VOTE OF THE PEOPLE? OBVIOUSLY SOMETHING'S
ROTTEN IN DENMARK. WE HAVE TO CHANGE THE FORM
OF OUR GOVERNMENT AND MOVE THE CAPITOL TO
ANCHORAGE OR PALMER.

In addition to the above basic components of an adverse possession
action, some courts require (by common law or statute), some or all of
the following:

- **Claim of title or claim of right. The Supreme Court of the
  United States has ruled that the mere intent to take the land
  as one's own constitutes "claim of right". Other cases have
  determined that a claim of right exists if the person believes
  he has rightful claim to the property, even if that belief is
  mistaken. A negative example would be a timber thief who
  sneaks onto a property, cuts timber not visible from the road,
  and hauls the logs away at night. His actions, though they
  demonstrate actual possession, also demonstrate knowledge
  of guilt, as opposed to claim of right.**
- **Good faith (in a minority of states) or bad faith (sometimes
  called the "Maine Rule" although it is now abolished in
  Maine)**
- **Improvement, cultivation, or enclosure**
- **Not under force of arms. Dispossession by armed invasion
  does not establish a claim of adverse possession against the
  true owner.**

When ANILCA was enacted a fifty-year moratorium was put in
place from 1959 to 2009 to settle land disputes before the natives could
get clear title to their lands. So when the fifty-year moratorium ended
the land disputes still had not been settled so the Legislature extended
it another 25-years thereby putting off for future generations to deal
with. The abolishment of squatter's rights/adverse possession laws have
no effect except to cause misery for people.

The people who used the land for generations and were supposed to receive ownership of their lands are excluded from their lands forever. The only people who benefited are the corporate officers who are drawing wages and their lawyers who keep on milking them for millions in legal fees--all to avoid paying the people who used the land for their very existence a few thousand dollars in compensation.

The Alaska native Land Claims Settlement Act specifically says: "... the land should go to the people who are living on it and using it for their smoke houses, drying racks, hunting and fishing camps, picking berries, etc." It does not discriminate against Whites or Indians.

We need judges who will uphold the law instead of looking for loopholes or making up new laws. I've seen politicians do everything in their power to avoid complying with the law.

ADVERSE POSSESSION

The doctrine of "adverse possession" is one of the most interesting in the field of real property law. The character of the law reflects the pioneer spirit of a growing world in both North America and Europe over the last few centuries.

If a person moves into possession of property, improves it and possesses it in a public manner, then after a certain amount of time he will acquire title to the property even though it is actually owned by someone else. The idea for adverse possession has at its root that land should not lie idle. If it does, it is wasted to the community. Therefore, if someone moves onto the land and makes it productive, that person may earn the right to claim it as his or her own. It is also reflective of the imprecise nature of ancient land sales: a person who believes he owns land, establishes himself on it in public, and is not hindered after a period of time, should be entitled to own the land.

The basic requirement for adverse possession is that the claiming party must take exclusive possession of the property. This type of possession is called "open and notorious" or proactive and absolutely not secretive possession. Some states require that the possession be "under color of title," or that the person must believe that he has the *right* to possess it *and* has some form of document or is relying on some fact that while not actually *conveying* title, appears to do so. In addition, many states require concurrent the payment of property taxes for a specified period of time, and a few states also require that improvements be made upon the land. Eventually, the possessor is required to file for title with the county recorder. The actual owner then has a limited amount of time in which to challenge the newcomer's title. Essentially, the owner's only argument is to claim some sort of disability; such as age, mental instability, or imprisonment. The owner is not required to do much in order to stop the possessor from acquiring title; merely sending the possessor a note granting permission to be there will usually suffice. Various rules exist regarding the continuousness of the possession and the ability to "tack" various periods of possession together in order to satisfy the time of possession requirement; see your state codes or the code of the state in which you are interested for more detailed information.

Adverse Possession list by state: (*Not enough room here to list every state.*)

ALASKA	09.45.052	and Color of Title: 7 yrs.	Not required but is considered proof *Alaska*

CHAPTER TWELVE

How Elites Bamboozle the World

The majority of the population in developed countries was bamboozled by the banksters and the Elites. How? Simple. In the past they did it by RELIGION. They enrolled everyone in a church, as a baby, by BAPTISM. Baptism makes you a Christian, who is SUBJECT to Catholic Church's law, the Canon law. So you became Church's SUBJECT for an empty promise of eternal life. Empty, because they never have to deliver on that.

So if the Canon law said that heretics are to be tortured or burned at the stake then the Church could LEGALLY do that to any Christian, without racking up bad karma. Only if they applied it to non-Christians, then they'd be breaking God's law and so accumulating bad karma.

But since a few hundred years ago, people would wise up and create SECULAR governments whose laws supersede the religious Canon law, the Elites needed something new to control the people. So they invented BIRTH CERTIFICATES.

Mind you, in a REPUBLIC there's no need for those since public records, such as hospital records, and births recorded in a family bible are proofs of citizenship. So what exactly are Birth Certificates? They're evidence of MEMBERSHIP in a PRIVATE limited-liability society. In

US that society is the federal gov't (United States). BTW, United States is NOT the nation, it means the FEDERAL GOV'T. See the Gold Reserve Act of 1934: (SEC. 15. "As used in this Act the term "United States" means the Government of the United States; the term "the continental United States "means the States of the United States, the District of Columbia, and the Territory of Alaska; the term "currency of the United States "means currency which is legal tender in the United States, and includes United States notes,")

Reading this section also tells you that "currency of the United States "means currency which is legal tender in the GOVERNMENT of United States. And that gov't is the FEDERAL GOV'T who's jurisdiction is ONLY over District of Columbia and territories. So "currency of the United States" is an INTERNAL currency of the federal gov't, that is NOT LEGAL TENDER outside of United States, i.e. in states of the Union. So it's NOT a national currency of the USA, especially since Congress was NOT granted power to issue bills of credit based on the debt it borrowed from private bankers.

Just think about it, why would a parent need to sign anything when his/hers baby is born? Doctor's signature and hospital record are plenty to prove a birth, especially since in the past only a bible record was needed to prove a birth.

And ALTERNATIVELY, the father/mother could simply sign THEIR OWN statement that their child was born at a certain place at certain time, and give it to the hospital personal. So if you got some babies coming soon, you could just do that. And if they insist that you MUST sign their birth certificate form, then obviously the BC is NOT a simple proof of birth, but is something more than that, such as the MEMBERSHIP in a private society, like I mentioned.

And of course membership in an association can be CANCELLED at any time, especially one where the terms weren't fully disclosed before signing. So you can simply end your US citizenship by CANCELLING IT. I'd also question any presumption that I was born under federal jurisdiction, by specifying that I was born in a state of the Union and not in any area subject to United States.

A friend of mine was brought into court for attempted murder. The case was bogus as the people who accused him were trying to get him fired from their corporation. When the Judge asked him for his identification he brought out his birth certificate written by his mother on birch bark. It was never registered with the government department of vital statistics. The court could not put an administrative trust on his birth bond because there was no bond to take money out of. No charges could be levied on his bond so the court could not get any money from his corporation. They had to dismiss the case.

MAKE ALASKA GREAT AGAIN

The pipeline was built between 1974 and 1977 after the 1973 oil crisis caused a sharp rise in oil prices in the United States. This rise made exploration of the Prudhoe Bay oil field economically feasible. Environmental, legal, and political debates followed the discovery of oil at Prudhoe Bay in 1968, and the pipeline was built only after the oil crisis provoked the passage of legislation designed to remove legal challenges to the project.

In building the pipeline, engineers faced a wide range of difficulties, stemming mainly from the extreme cold and the difficult, isolated terrain. The construction of the pipeline was one of the first large-scale projects to deal with problems caused by permafrost, and special construction techniques had to be developed to cope with the frozen ground. The project attracted tens of thousands of workers to Alaska, causing a boomtown atmosphere in Valdez, Fairbanks, and Anchorage.

The first barrel of oil traveled through the pipeline in 1977, and full-scale production began by the end of the year. Several notable incidents of oil leakage have occurred since, including those caused by sabotage, maintenance failures, and bullet holes. As of 2010, the pipeline had shipped almost 16 billion barrels of oil. At an average price of $72 per barrel that would equal on trillion 152 billion dollars. Where do you suppose all that money went? It certainly didn't build many roads and infrastructure.

The service life of the Trans-Alaska pipeline was estimated to be twenty-five years. At the present time the pipeline is 40 years old. As volumes decrease, Alyeska will begin closing pump stations. The company intends to close all but four stations, because the lower throughput will require less pumping to maintain its momentum. While some reports supporting drilling in the ANWR coastal plain maintain that the pipeline may reach its minimum operating level of 200,000 barrels per day by 2020. The Trans-Alaska Pipeline System Renewal Environmental Impact Statement estimated levels above this through at least 2032 due to ongoing exploration outside ANWR.

This estimate is far too optimistic. Pipelines do not last 100-years because sulfuric acids and abrasive particles in the oil (tars sands) eat through the metal. I t could shut down any time.

Time to speak out, by Ed Martin *Ediro's note* Ed is a contractor and his father was one of Alaska's original homesteaders.*

President Dwight D. Eisenhower signed the Alaska Statehood Act into United States law on July 4, 1958. That 4th of July was special to most Alaskans, even to this day! The 4th of July is a National/State day of freedom, guaranteeing us all liberty as individuals. With that, we all had courage to break the soil and build this great state.

Now 60 years later I don't find as much wisdom being used to carry us forward. Why is that? What is holding us back? We aren't lazy. It must be something else holding us back. Have we looked at what we possess? The millions of acres and abundant resources that sit idle in government hands not creating jobs, opportunity, and new wealth so we can improve ourselves, our families, neighbors and communities? The land is the key to our success and now is the time we should be making good of the statehood dreams and promises stipulated in the state Constitution. Our Constitution's stated policy "encourages the settlement of its lands", but in a manner that recognizes the people as the "owners" of these lands and resources! They currently need to recognize the need at this time to sell enough land to families to carry out the task of making the state a self-sustainable. We shouldn't have to wait for another century to realize this promise!

According to the March 12, Clarion Alaska lost 8,900 citizens last year. In December 7000 Syrians immigrated to Alaska. That means Alaska actually lost 15,900 residents. Over twenty-thousand people will leave Alaska next year if nothing is done to get more land into private hands and finish the road to Nome. It was surveyed in 1944. **It Isn't fair that our government is sitting on trillions of dollars in land and resources yet insists on taxing citizens, taking the PFD and driving tens of thousands of its citizens out of state.** The 2017 Kenai Borough delinquent tax list totals $2,158,019.16 and will be much more next year. If people had money from raising crops and mining they could pay their taxes and feed themselves.

My plan is not a total solution but it renews our spirit, gives us opportunity by utilizes our resources, and creates new wealth. Some think that we have an unsustainable budget however, it's well within our means to save state jobs, pay out a full PFD and create new wealth with some wisdom as I mentioned above. **Land ownership and tending livestock will keep our grandchildren off the street and out of prison. You can't have a free state without land ownership. We're all in this together.**

If our government would allow citizens to own one acre of land equal to the value of one PFD. It's called the principal of "equity of scale." A value needs to be established for the trade and what has us divided. All Alaskans can benefit from this reconciliation of the past and trust in our government. If this plan is implemented with 200,000 - 5-acre parcels the Kenai Borough will have lots of money to fund schools and roads.

Our government took half our PFD. That amount applied to the value of the land at the average price per acre of $1,600.00. Henry Kroll thinks it should be $1000 an acre due to the fact that people not able to pay their property tax. The trade in equity is at least one acre to all Alaskans per PFD check. Parcels of land are requested individually on a first come first served basis. The timeframe is 2 years to redeem your Alaska Land Voucher.

Mining properties could see settlement making them more productive, and fishing/guide sites & tourism sites could be expanded where there is private ownership. The time has come to feel the freedom our fathers, dreamed of. Let's do this together for all of our benefit especially future generations. Best wishes, Henry Kroll, Ed Martin, Jr. & Family

Henry Kroll

President, Donald Trump
The White House
Washington, DC 20500

Dear Mr. President;

You have 713 military bases in 197 countries around the world. I think we should bring about half of our boys' home to help rebuild the infrastructure in the US.

Here in Alaska we need to finish the road to Nome and possibly have a ferry system or tunnel to Russia. I believe the Russians would fund part of the expenses. This would increase trade and quadruple tourism as it would allow up to drive across Russia to Europe. The value of such a road for tourism and trade would be in calculable.

F.Y.I. We wouldn't have a road to Alaska if the Japanese hadn't made a diversionary attempt to invade in WWII. I wrote you two previous letters about this. The government of Alaska is broke and facing a 3-billion dollar a year budget shortfall. There is no way they can fix it. The reason they are broke is they were greedy and didn't think ahead and allowed big corporations with their professional negotiators' to make deals to tap non-renewable resources. Now the only oil pipeline is running at ¼ capacity and the people responsible are retired and living in Palm Springs.

If a road is ever going to be built it has to be constructed by either by the US government or the military. Alaska is considered to be a military reservation. The best way to get the job done is have the military build it because it would eliminate some of the environment opposition. It would give the Army something constructive to do without getting shot at.

Sincerely, Henry Kroll

To:
Governor, Mike Dunleavy
PO Box 110001
Juneau, Alaska 99811

RE: Alaska's concentration camps:

Dear Governor Mike Dunleavy:
    In the course of my daily book research I came across some startling statics. The Department of Corrections figures: as of December 1, 2012, list the number of Alaska Native Alaskans in prison compared with other races in Alaska as 66.08 % statewide. Over half the prison populations are native Alaskans. The 2010 census lists Alaska's total Native population as 14.8 percent. It's all about "charging" them with something to take their land and birth bonds. The Judges and Prosecutors get a percentage of the many millions of dollars taken. They also keep the Permanent Fund dividend checks. Public policy is about money.
    The number of Alaska Native women in Alaska's prisons is 75.94 percent compared with other races yet the total native population is only 14.8%.. Do you see the disparity here? Did Native women write the laws? Did Native men and women write the State Constitution? Other occupied nations around the world don't lock up so many of their indigenous populations. Why are so many native women being sterilized? Are they trying to reduce the indigenous populations?
    Alaska has a higher demographic percentage of indigenous people in prison than any other nation in the world. Alaska is a military occupation state.

I think you should show this letter to your wife and get her opinion on this matter. I also think you should form a taskforce to look into this matter.

The Mormon Church has this figured out decades ago. Have you ever been to the Polynesian Cultural Center in Hawaii? It's a big university theme park funded by tourism. People come from all over the world to see and study it. Students who work there come from all the different tribes around the Pacific. Each individual tribe has a replica of the type of dwellings their ancestors lived in. Students demonstrate crafts like making fire etc.

This was very educational for me because I could understand why some of the buildings were constructed that way. Some were only huts but some were magnificently made to impress people. Once the invading war party set foot on the beach and observed thirty-foot tall buildings with elaborately carved decorations the invaders knew that the people that they intended to rob and kill were more advanced than their primitive war party. Instead of killing they desired to know more about how to live their luxurious life style. Tahitian drums are really something to hear.

This state has three-million acres on the Kenai Peninsula. Why not set aside a couple hundred acres bordering a small lake for a University that allows all students to get their CDL's, computer skills, pilot licenses, marksmanship, gun safety, heavy equipment operation, mechanics, welding, cooking, carpentry, construction, oil recover, well drilling and demonstrate their Native culture?

Such skill as tanning hides, bead work, ivory carving, tool making, flute and drum making, jewelry etc. All these skills are still necessary in today's world. Tourists could paddle dugout canoes with outriggers much like they do in Hawaii. Other examples of water craft could be Eskimo skin boats covered with canvas or plastic instead of walrus hide.

Each tribe could have a replica of the dwellings their ancestors lived in—much like the Polynesian Cultural Center. Each tribe could have replicas of the tools they used in daily life etc. The students get paid minimum wage. When they graduate they can live with a feeling of hope instead of hopelessness and futility. They will know their culture and how to survive and how to cope with today's modern society.

Large hydroponic greenhouses and farm animals would provide most of the food. If it were built near the natural gas line along the k-beach road the costs would be less. Getting people out of prison to become productive members of society would save the state money.

Each of the Native Corporations should fund a portion of this University project. It will have to have dorms and classrooms but the state should not fund the entire program. If you asked the BIA and other Federal agencies I am sure they would help contribute money. Private donations would also contribute some of the money. This is only one small step in the right direction. Baby steps...

Sincerely, Henry Kroll

We are no longer a resource state. The Nome gold rush of the 1890's to present day plus Kennecott Copper took most of the copper and gold. They dug up a copper nugget the size of a Volkswagen. They discovered a copper nugget too big to lift at the bottom of the pit.

The oil pipeline is running at 20 % and state4 spending has run amok. Rather they realize it or not the economic engine of the future OF Alaska are the Native Corporations.

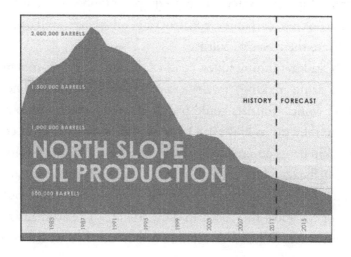

When that 40-year old Trans Alaska pipeline with a service life of 25 years currently running at one-quarter capacity starts springing leaks we're in big trouble. The State will have to shut it down and the Permanent Fund will be used to clean up the mess. Everything is in fraud.

Currently only one percent of the land in Alaska is privately owned and the state constitution is set up so that the people don't own land. Everything belongs to the state. This state is killing our children with the **'Public Policy'** of removing ingenious populations from their lands to claim resources to enrich big corporations. This creates a cycle of poverty, alcohol and drug abuse, crime and suicide among our young of all colors because they have no hope! They have no place to go! Once you take native people from their motherland they are like vessels adrift on the sea with no anchor. They don't know where to go and how to provide for themselves and wind up living on the street. **Land ownership provides that anchor!**

Every year universities keep pumping out more people with degrees to fill non-productive bureaucrat jobs. Our sovereignty and freedom has been stolen by the government's "public policy" of **engineered recidivism** to keep public servants employed.

Land ownership is essential for sovereignty and freedom. Native Elders should take some of the blame for neglecting the kids. They live in relative luxury on money from the village corporations and refuse to change their ways. Land ownership is tantamount to grow food. The government representatives know this so why aren't they doing something about it? If the food supply were interrupted from the lower 48-states by war or if Yellowstone Caldera erupts we are all in grave danger of starving to death. Only two percent of the food consumed in Alaska is grown in Alaska. Our Kenai Peninsula Borough alone is sitting on 750,000 acres near Gray Cliff Subdivision and the state is sitting on 3-million acres (not counting the land across Cook Inlet, the mountains behind Port Graham, Seldovia and Homer) that could be used to produce food such as fish, chickens, ducks, geese, goats, sheep, cattle and root crops. We need our children to take care of livestock to gain work experience.

While living on the street our children forget their language, culture and survival skills. If the alcohol and drugs don't kill them depression, prostitution and suicide will. The current **'public policy'** is a terrible crime and a waste of human lives. It is also a violation of animist **religious beliefs**. While living on the street they get busted for drugs and wind up with a criminal record and never get out of the circle of poverty. This creates non-productive jobs for more police, prison guards, judges, psychiatrists, prosecutors, parole officers, lawyers, dope dealers etc., etc. This is engineered recidivism to keep people on the government payroll.

Denying indigenous populations the right to eat natural foods forces them to eat genetically modified food guaranteeing to shorten their lifespan with diabetes and is eugenics. It is a form of healthcare slavery that forces them to stay in town close to doctors. They aren't allowed to travel far to hunt and fish. Slavery is a theft of life, freedom and labor. The State's solution is to build more clinics and hire more bureaucrats which is a crime against native peoples. The enemy is larger than GMOs; it's more related to the multinational corporations.

Children in Alaska get up between ten and noon and sneak over to a friend's house to inhale vapes or smoke pot. State and federal regulation prevent them from working so they get in trouble. They eat genetically modified foods laced with Roundup and other pesticides guaranteed to give them diabetes to create jobs for healthcare professionals. I am convinced this **"Public policy"** is engineered to create more jobs for people with degrees in counseling and drug rehabilitation jobs.

The government's idea to solve the problem is to build drug rehabilitation and abortion clinics and hire more civil service employees. They don't care about what they are doing to future generations. Most of the people that go into drug rehab clinics wind up back on the street. Politicians are using our young as sex slaves to create jobs for bureaucrats. We are dealing with psychopaths who have no moral restraint in causing the death of one person or a million. The only solution is to rescue the human society with native values of life.

Children in the rest of the world milk cows, goats and feed livestock. They learn responsibility and work ethic. They don't have to drink pasteurized milk laced with growth hormones and estrogen that causes early maturation in both males and females to rob them of their sexuality. Now we have a whole new generation of gender-neutral boys that are not likely to reproduce and the girls are being injected with Gardisol rendering them sterile.

We have to go back to the old ways to teach our young how to grow food, hunt, fish and care for livestock. If we don't, the future is doomed. Our schools need to teach how to farm tomatoes, potatoes, rutabagas and milk goats instead of useless IT degrees. A war or EMP will destroy the internet and computers everywhere. If you get a group of kids together to where some of them get excited about these skills peer pressure will make the rest follow.

Without being exposed to the TEN COMMANDMENTS and the GOLDEEN RULE kids have no basis to determine right from wrong. Parents, teachers and the church needs to do their part to instill moral guidance and explain how mankind survived through the ages using natural and COMMON LAW. This will stop the government's plan of population reduction and engineered recidivism to keep the jails full.

Over the years I have come to the conclusion ALASKA doesn't want a middle class. It wants a population dependent on government handouts that will vote for the next big corporate sale of resources so they can take in billions of dollars and spend it on building more government instead of infrastructure that would actually benefit the people. We are being held captive and few people understand this. What are we going to do when all the resources are gone?

MEMORANDUM IN SUPPORT

Empty oil tankers returning to Alaska must take on ballast water in order to run in the open ocean otherwise they could roll over. For twenty-five years the State of Alaska allowed over a hundred oil tankers a year to each dump 10 to 20-million gallons of algae and sewage contaminated ballast water taken from Los Angeles, Honolulu and Anacortes Washington boat harbors and pump it into lower Cook Inlet. The tankers start discharging ballast water when they reach the entrance of Cook Inlet. By the time they get to the oil storage facilities the ballast water has been discharged and they are ready to take on oil. Twenty-million gallons of ballast water from 600 oil tankers a year totals about 120,000,000,000 –that's over one-hundred twenty-billion gallons a year. In ten years they dumped 200 billion gallons. Note* Many algae can double in number every twelve hours.

It took twenty years to destroy the crab and shrimp fisheries. Twenty years of dumping toxic waste plus the city of Anchorage dumping another, ten-millions of gallons of sewage a day into upper Cook Inlet and twenty years of offshore oil wells dumping radioactive drill tailing and drilling mud, the shrimp, crab and clams were exterminated.

When I was young I could walk down any beach in Seldovia bay wearing hip-boots and my pants would get wet from clams squirting water three feet in the air. You could look into the sun along the beach you would see hundreds of water jets spouting like a fountain. The clams were so big and healthy that they couldn't close their shells. You only had to dig a hole, the size of a five-gallon buck to get half a bucket of clams. The beaches were alive. There were centipedes, snails, worms and everything was moving. Now the beaches are dead. There is nothing. It's a sad state of affairs when you can't trust your government to take care of your resources!

Shrimp, crab and clams are bivalves. After their eggs hatch the spat must swim to the surface in the spring to feed on the first plankton bloom. When the ecosystem had been altered by contaminates such as bacteria and algae that suck up all the oxygen the plankton dies. The entire ecosystem is poisoned by chemicals, plastics and heavy metals in solution. Add to this a layer of oil on the surface that suffocates zooplankton and you have a recipe for disaster. I believe our food supply was purposely poisoned for the purpose of getting rid of most commercial fishermen so there would be less opposition to future offshore drilling. Practically all the shrimp and crab were exterminated.

To add insult to injury the state blamed the depletion of the resource on the fishermen. Many fishermen like myself, lost their boats, wives, houses and everything. The loss of my livelihood cost me several million dollars.

The state wanted to get rid of commercial fisherman so they could sell billions of dollars in oil leases in lower Cook Inlet south of Kaligan Island and in Kachemak Bay. They had visions of grandeur making it look like the Gulf of Mexico will oil rigs in every direction from horizon to horizon. Oil companies weren't interested in dealing with Alaska's bureaucracy so very few oil leases were sold.

Due to state greed the people living in the cities of Homer, Seldovia and Kodiak were cheated out of their livelihood and a billion dollars that went into the private sector. I was forced to fish further west out of Kodiak and eventually wound up fishing out of King Cove in order to earn enough money to support my family. Being away from home for months at a time and the stress of trying to make a living with an old 76-foot boat Mary M built in 1929 when the resource was declining resulted in my divorce.

When the forty+-year-old pipeline starts springing leaks, the carpet beggars who came here to get rich will scurry away likes rats leaving a singing ship to go back to the hell holes they came out of.

CRIMINAL MANAGEMENT OF RESOURCES

So far the Swan Lake fire cost more than 46-million dollars and it is still burning. According to a US forest Service radio announcement forest fires consume 2000 square miles in Alaska every year --probably more this year. There is no excuse. This year Alaska and Federal governments spent about 200-million dollars fighting fires. In addition, Alaskans have to buy practically all our building material from Canada and other states to build a house. There is no excuse for wasting millions of dollars when a portion of that could be spent on building roads and fire breaks.

When a large fire like the Swan Lake fire breaks out the dry smoke and dust causes additional lightning strikes that cause more fires. Why won't the government accept this fact?

Forests are public owned resources managed by government. Residents should be allowed to construct fire breaks for the purpose of harvesting trees for cabins, lumber and firewood. Instead government let forests burn wasting hundreds of millions of dollars, worth of lumber and house logs. Their management philosophy is an inflexible, authoritarian, ideology prompted by pseudo environmentalists. We need more residents managing state resources instead of Dudley Dorights abiding by some United Nations agreement.

USFWS Federal land managers posted a report that shows how out of touch they are. "One of the five main purposes of the refuge is "…to fulfill the international obligations of the United States with respect to fish and wildlife and their inhabitants." According to them, prohibiting the initial attack on the fire meets an international obligation. How can160-thoousand acres of burning forest that was sprayed with water and fertilizer washing downstream into the Kenai River system to alter the food chain killing off salmon fry can be an international obligation?

The report goes on to say: "The suppression of wild land fire is an attempt by humans to interrupt the native cycle of disturbance. "These fires are wild by their very nature; they are difficult to predict and often difficult to rein in this natural process for the benefit of human populations." Government management is the enemy of nature! Forest fires cause ash clouds that cause more lightning strikes that cause more forest fires!

The report went to comment about the air quality and the smog. According to them humanity is the enemy of nature. The Swan Lake fire degraded the air quality all summer. Besides the direct costs of over 46-million dollars it cost south central Alaska probably another100-million dollars. It took ten days for the Feds to enlist fire fighters to manage the fire. By that time it exposed a pipeline shutting down the major highway. It burnt the Bradley lake transmission lines that furnish power to Anchorage. Electrical rate payers will pay higher utilities bills for months to come. The fire caused a plane to crash with the loss of three lives.

Divide 160-thousand acres by number of acres in a square mile 640 you get 250-square miles of charcoal. If that land were divided into 160 acre homesteads you would have 1000 homesteads—enough to supply most of the food for Alaska. Only 2-percet of the food we eat is grown here. Greedy bureaucrats have put us in danger. If a war or other natural disaster like an EMP or draught should interrupt food production in the lower states we could die! There is no excuse for not allowing the public to develop and manage natural resources to create a self-sustaining State.

Governments sell resources to big corporations and use the money to build more government instead of roads for the people. After the state sells all the oil and gas and allows the feds to burn the forests how will our grandchildren survive? We must demand the Federal government pay us for our losses and demand that we get more local control of our forests and all our natural resources.

"It's just like the Vietnam War; students have got to speak up and save us from this criminal government." –Sophie Murray Age 18, graduate of Kenai Central High School.

Download my free books to discover the real cause of the destruction of the fisheries. Government management! www.GuardDogBooks.com

How can we fix Alaska?

1. Make our elected leaders adhere to their oaths of office by enacting a statute to cut their pay one month for each violation.
2. Get more land into the private sector so that we are not so dependent on other states for practically everything. This will make us safer and create more jobs.
3. Finish the road to Nome to make it possible for people to create wealth and trade with Russia.

MAKE ALASKA GREAT AGAIN

Alaskan's are in grave danger. Make Alaska Great again is about making more land and resources available for Alaskan's so that they are not 100% dependent on other states for everything. At the present time if Alaska misses two shipments of food from the lower states people will starve. What if a war or revolution starts in the lower forty-eight States or an EMP from the Sun, or extreme draught due to climate change or Yellowstone Volcano erupting destroys most of the food crops, no food will be shipped to Alaska. We can't depend on Russia for aid.

This book is about saving the state from a fate similar to Argentina where the government controls all the resources and sells them and wastes the money creating more government. Alaska's current administration takes in more money per capita than any other state and uses the money to create more government. It needs to build a road to Nome like was planned during WWII to allow citizens access to resources. A ferry system to Russia would boost tourism and trade.

We need to give up that childish Cold War and stop pointing nukes at each other. Mutually assured destruction is insane! Why keep on spending billions to maintain old junk that probably to rusty to detonate?

Ask yourself what are we and our grandchildren going to do after the state destroys all the renewable resources and sells off the rest? Their track record of management of renewable resources speaks for itself...

Henry Kroll was born in the tiny fishing village of Seldovia, Alaska. After attending University of Alaska and Sheldon Jackson Jr. College and University of Corpus Christi, Texas, Henry fished king crab 23 years catching over 3-million pounds and the same amount of snow crab. Henry Kroll now has more than 13,000 days as Captain in command of various vessels. Every July and August he fished commercial salmon set-nets on the west side of Cook Inlet 65 years harvesting more than two million pounds.

Henry is author of twelve books on advanced science, politics, government corruption and Alaskan Legends. Henry became involved in writing because of his strong interest in longevity, science, and the light source that made the coal, oil and limestone on Earth from carbon dioxide.

Henry used all fields of science to discover that our Sun was born in Orion and was captured by the Sirius A and B, a white dwarf star that puts out more than 100 times the light of our sun. Our sun didn't make the carbon energy on this planet because early Earth's 750 PSI carbon dioxide atmosphere was 2,800 miles deep. You would never see the sun with such an atmosphere. COSMOLOGICAL ICE AGES is the greatest detective story ever.

Henry's books can be found at www.GuardDogBooks.com and www. Amazon.com and www.AmazonUK.com For COSMOLOGICAL ICE AGES wholesale orders go: www.trafford.com